Charlie Palmer's

Casual Cooking

Other Books by Charlie Palmer with Judith Choate

Great American Food

Charlie Palmer

with Judith Choate

Charlie Palmer's

Casual Cooking

The Chef of New York's Aureole Restaurant Cooks for Family and Friends

William Morrow
An Imprint of HarperCollins*Publishers*

For my sons:
Courtland, Randall, Eric, and Reed—
You make our family table complete

HarperCollins books may be purchased for educational, business, or sales promotional use. For information please write: Special Markets Department, HarperCollins Publishers Inc., 10 East 53rd Street, New York, NY 10022.

FIRST EDITION

Designed by Ralph L. Fowler

Printed on acid-free paper

Library of Congress Cataloging-in-Publication Data
Palmer, Charlie, 1959–
    [Casual cooking]
    Charlie Palmer's casual cooking : the chef of New York's Aureole Restaurant cooks for family and friends / Charlie Palmer.— 1st ed.
        p.   cm.
    ISBN 0-688-17873-1
    1. Cookery.   I. Title.

TX714 .P348   2001
641.5—dc21   00–041882

00 01 02 03 04 FF 10 9 8 7 6 5 4 3 2 1

Contents

Acknowledgments   vii

Introduction   1

The Well-Stocked Kitchen   5

A Group of Soups   **11**

All Kinds of Salads   **39**

Lunch and Brunch   **67**

Vegetables and Sides   **103**

Pasta and Risotto   **125**

Poultry and Game Birds   **137**

Meat and Game   **159**

Seafood   **187**

Desserts   **203**

Sources   235

Index   237

Acknowledgments

For inspiration, memorable family gatherings, great meals, love, and support:

My parents, Joyce and Dwight—you are deeply missed.

My late brother, David

Neil and Veronica Palmer

Brenda, Bill, and Sadie Michaels

Spike and Vicki Lamoreaux

Leslie and Lois Palmer

My grandmothers, Nannie Marguerite Palmer and Hazel Lee—you set the example.

Doc and Rosemary Villarini and all of the Villarini siblings and their families

Sharon Crain and Connie Wright and all of my friends in Smyrna

And, of course, Lisa, who is always by my side.

With gratitude:

To the staff of each restaurant, past and present, in the kitchen and at the front of the house—your skill has made it possible for me to catch these moments with my family.

To Justin Schwartz, Harriet Bell, Karen Ferries, Carrie Weinberg, and the marvelous crew at William Morrow for helping to bring the book alive.

And to Gozen Koshida and Hiromi Hayashi for the mouthwatering photographs of our home table.

Introduction

For most of my life, I've done my cooking in restaurants. But in recent years, following marriage and the speedy arrival of four sons, cooking at home has become a necessity. Because I am always in my restaurants during the week, home cooking with and for my family and friends usually happens on Saturdays and Sundays. Who has time to cook during the week these days? For most of us, the weekend is when we take the time to make special meals. And although we may love to eat good food and to enjoy it with family and friends, no one, especially me, wants to spend the entire weekend in the kitchen. For me, this means, easy-to-prepare main courses that can spin off into other meals.

Whether in my restaurants or at home, I always cook seasonally because ingredients harvested at their peak are at their absolute best. But beyond this, I've always felt that my appetite has a time clock that stops and goes when it is fed with something wonderful from whatever season is emerging. I know that it is March when I begin to yearn for crisp, barely cooked, pencil-slim asparagus, gently sweet, buttery soft-shell crabs or shad roe, and greens that sprout with the first hint of warmth—pea shoots, cress, spinach. My appetite turns with the seasons, heralding each change with sensory demands that must be fed. With today's bounty of greenmarkets, farmers' markets, roadside stands, specialty food stores, and well-stocked supermarkets, I know I can always fill my seasonal demands.

As I began cooking at home for four hungry boys, I had to rethink my style. They didn't want and I didn't have the time to cook my restaurant-style meals, so I found myself looking back to the home-cooked meals of my childhood for inspiration. And I can assure you that it was only for inspiration, since my mom was like many cooks of her generation who were delighted to welcome newcomers like Duncan Hines, Betty Crocker, and the Green Giant into their kitchens. Oh, we did have meat loaf, pot roast, meatballs and spaghetti, biscuits, and chocolate layer cakes—they just came, either totally or in part, from prepared mixes or cans or boxes.

When well made, those comfort foods from the past are truly memorable, and I can't think of anything I like better. But the marketplace has changed so dramatically that you can, by simply shopping in a neighborhood supermarket, invent your own comfort food. My weekend meals brim with flavor yet have all of the warmth of Mom's cooking. Sometimes it is simply a matter of updating an old favorite with now-available ingredients, but as often as not it is putting ingredients together in a whole new, yet comfortable way.

I know, perhaps better than most, how difficult it can be to create wonderful meals every day, so when I cook at home, I want my kitchen time to be relaxed and effortless. At home, instead of my kitchen brigade and prep cooks, I have, just like many home cooks, young children vying to be my assistants. This doesn't make cooking easy, but it sure does make it fun. Unlike many home cooks, though, I am often able to bring home stocks, prepped vegetables, and premium meats from the restaurant, but the recipes in this book require none of these as I know that most home cooks don't have such luxuries at hand. All of the ingredients used here, with perhaps one or two exceptions, are available at almost any supermarket, but also shop at farmers' markets, roadside stands, and small specialty shops, where you can support local producers and growers.

To me, shopping for the weekend is often as much of an adventure as cooking. On Saturday morning, my boys, Courtland, Randall, Eric, and Reed, and I visit one or more of the extraordinary food markets in our neighborhood or, if we are in the country, our nearby farm stands, so I can see what's available, reasonably priced, and enticing and the boys can make sure that dessert will be on the menu. I don't have to tell you how expensive grocery shopping can be, but trained in the French manner, I always try to make sure that I am going to use all that I buy. Waste, more than extravagance, costs in the kitchen. I would much rather spend money on the best that I can buy for a particular recipe (and most recipes don't require a premium cut of meat or exotic fruits or vegetables) and then make sure that I can use all of it in one way or another than to buy cheaply. And yet, a bargain basket of summer's bounty—you can always freeze or preserve—or an extra-large bag of any kitchen staple is, to me, an economy.

Weekend cooking is, in many ways, no different from what I do in the restaurant. Even though I might be cooking a one-pot meal or working outdoors on the grill, I still think about taste, texture, and presentation. Since we eat with both our eyes and our mouths, I want the finished plates to be as enticing as the aromas and flavors that come from the pan. This is really just a matter of recollection—thinking about memorable meals and then re-creating them in my kitchen. For instance, I often recall one of the meals of my childhood that was particularly comforting, then bring it to our family table with my own stamp on it.

I'm crazy about deep, rich flavors, which I find especially easy to extract when braising and stewing. Equally, I appreciate the clean, clearly defined taste of a simple grill or roast. These are techniques that I use over and over again as I cook at home. Some of the dishes in this book are quick and easy to make. Others take some time and effort and are, perhaps, best left to the long holiday weekends, when the pleasure of cooking is shared with guests. But I think that every recipe will be one that you will go back to time after time, as I do.

The best thing about cooking this way is that you can often prepare more than one meal at a time. The Perfect Roast Chicken (page 138) doesn't create leftovers, it makes a scrumptious Aïoli Chicken Salad (page 63), or chicken salad BLTs, or Mom's Chicken Noodle Soup (page 34). When you've prepared a big batch of Charlie's Famous Corn Chowder (page 12), the cup and a half that remains after everyone's had his fill can be pureed to make the base for a cream soup or a sauce. Nothing ever goes to waste in the hands of a well-seasoned weekend cook!

We never have fancy hors d'oeuvres or appetizers at home, even when guests are coming. In the summer, my wife, Lisa, might arrange a basket of freshly picked vegetables for which I might make a low-calorie dip to serve by the pool with drinks. Or winters might find a bowl of nuts in their shells (you can't believe how absolutely delicious roasted walnuts fresh from your oven can be), some cheese straws, or even a bowl of lightly salted mixed nuts, to be served with wine. Nothing elaborate. Nothing that takes time away from family and friends.

With a house full of rowdy boys and many pint-sized guests, I never prepare special meals for them. They eat what we eat, and even the picky eaters seem to do just fine. I like to think that this is because the food is simple and easy to eat and we don't make a fuss about it. It's just there for the eating.

Peanut butter and jelly is always on hand for the pickiest of the picky eaters, adult and child alike.

Cooking at home, even if it is only on weekends, is the stuff from which tradition is made. Memories of good old-fashioned home cooking serve as a remarkable equalizer, as each of us can recall some very special meals (even if, in afterthought, the food wasn't very good) that came from our mother's kitchen. There is no reason that we shouldn't be passing along homemade memories with homemade meals of our own.

I know I'm not unusual in this regard. There are many cooks, moms, dads, or singles, who have the time to cook only on weekends. What I do know is that if you plan your cooking schedule well, you will have meals on hand for at least part of the week, and these home-cooked meals will be far more nutritious, tasty, and rewarding than the take-out alternatives.

Although I find myself with just enough time to cook at home on weekends, I offer favorite recipes that you will want to cook every day. Each dish can be served with confidence at the family table, for a group of close friends, or when you want to entertain for a special event. And, since many of these once everyday foods are now infrequently served, you will find them quite special additions to your table. I am delighted to have you join my family and friends around our table—we love sharing our good food and good fortune with friends.

The Well-Stocked Kitchen

For easy cooking, you should have the best-quality kitchen equipment on hand. When a home cook asks, I always recommend buying the best pots and pans available. AllClad, Lincoln Centurion by Wearever, Sitram, and Calphalon brands are four that I can suggest. If you invest just once in heavy-duty pots and pans with tight-fitting lids, fine-quality nonstick baking pans, the right size frying and sauté pans for ease of handling, professional-quality electrical appliances such as KitchenAid's, chef-quality knives such as Henckels, Global, or Wüsthof, and stainless steel and Pyrex bowls and measuring equipment, your kitchen will be stocked for your entire cooking life.

Besides quality equipment, every kitchen should have some basic ingredients on hand at all times. All-purpose, whole wheat, semolina, and super-fine Wondra flours; granulated, light brown, and confectioners' sugars; baking powder and baking soda; fresh eggs and canned egg whites; freshly grated and frozen Parmesan, Romano, and/or Asiago cheeses; long-grain, brown, Arborio (or other Italian risotto rice), and basmati rices; dried pastas such as thin spaghetti and cappellini as well as shaped pastas; canned Italian plum tomatoes; extra virgin and regular olive oils; unflavored oils such as canola or peanut; red wine, white wine, and balsamic vinegars; dried fruits such as raisins and apricots; dried and canned beans such as cannellini, black, and kidney; smoked meats such as bacon and pancetta; the spices you commonly use; fresh onions and garlic; and walnuts and almonds are some of the stores that you should always find on your shelves. Your freezer should always contain some clarified butter, chopped herbs, roasted garlic, and, of course, vanilla ice cream. With these ingredients on hand, you will always be able to prepare a Friday night supper (or even a whole weekend of meals) without frantically running to the market.

Stocks

Almost all cookbooks by chefs recommend that you use homemade meat, poultry, shellfish, and vegetable stocks. Of course, I too believe that you will create the most flavorful dishes using homemade stocks; however, I also know that most home cooks do not have the time it takes to make an excellent stock. And, if you want to know a secret, I don't know any professional chefs who would spend their time off making a stock for home use. If they can't cart it home from the restaurant, they do the same thing most home cooks do—use commercially prepared broths. Although we all know that these are not as good as a rich home brew, there are now some fine-quality broths available. I have found Pacific Organic chicken, mushroom, and vegetable broths (available from many supermarkets and health food stores) to be quite good, but if you can't find that brand, the Healthy Request brand, available at most supermarkets, seems to be a good alternative. In addition, check your local health food store for high-quality unsalted, defatted broths and keep trying different ones until you find one that you like. (If you want to make a light meat broth, use three-quarters beef broth and one-quarter chicken broth.)

Roasted Garlic

Roasted garlic is another ingredient that adds a lot of flavor to many dishes, but with little effort. Whatever you don't use that day can be frozen. Freeze it, tightly wrapped in foil, some as whole heads and some broken apart into individual cloves, to make it easier to defrost the amount you need.

For easy removal of the garlic pulp after roasting, cut off the top third of each head to bare the flesh. To roast garlic, coat the whole head or individual cloves with olive oil, wrap the garlic in aluminum foil, and roast it in a pan in a preheated 325°F oven for about 1 hour, or until the flesh is very soft when pierced with a knife.

For a more aromatic roast, cut off the top third of whole heads as above and place them in a shallow baking dish with enough chicken or vegetable broth to cover them by one-third. Add any herbs that you like—thyme and rosemary are particularly good. Drizzle olive oil over each head and season to taste with salt and pepper. Leave the pan uncovered and bake as above.

Roasted Peppers

Red, green, yellow, and purple bell peppers (the purple ones turn green when exposed to heat) can be roasted on an open stove-top flame, in a preheated 450°F oven, under a preheated broiler, or on a gas, charcoal, or wood-fired grill. Wash them well and roast, turning frequently, for about 20 minutes, or until the skin is totally blackened. Remove and place them in a resealable plastic bag. Seal and allow the peppers to steam for about 10 minutes. When cool enough to handle, remove the peppers from the bag and, using your fingers, peel and discard the skins from the peppers. Cut lengthwise in half and remove the core, seeds, and membranes. Leave in halves or cut into slices. Store, tightly covered and refrigerated, for up to 3 days. Or marinate the peppers in olive oil, a touch of red wine or balsamic vinegar, some roasted garlic, and salt and pepper to taste. In the marinade, they will keep, tightly covered and refrigerated, for 1 week.

Fresh Herbs

Almost every supermarket now carries fresh herbs year-round. The flavor of fresh herbs is subtler and less astringent than dried ones and that makes a huge difference in the final taste of a dish. If you buy a bunch of fresh herbs and are going to use only a tablespoon or so, or you have an abundance of garden-fresh herbs, freeze them in plastic containers for future use.

When basil starts to overtake my garden in August, I cut it back and puree the leaves with just enough olive oil to make a thick puree. Then I measure it out by the tablespoonful, wrap each portion in plastic, place the little bundles in a resealable plastic bag labeled with the name and date, and freeze. This method prevents waste in the garden and gives me a fresh basil taste all winter. All soft herbs can be frozen in this fashion. Hardier herbs such as rosemary can be frozen on their stems. Just make sure you label them before putting them in the freezer.

Clarified Butter

Clarified butter does not burn as readily as whole butter, which makes it perfect for sautéing or frying when you want a rich butter flavor, and it is easy to prepare while you are working on something else in the kitchen. It is usually best to work with at least 1 pound of butter at a time. Place the butter in a heavy saucepan over low heat for about 30 minutes, skimming off the white froth as it forms. Raise the heat slightly and continue skimming until the remaining butter is clear, about 30 minutes longer. Do not allow the butter to simmer or boil, or it will be unusable. Remove the clarified butter from the heat and let it stand for about 15 minutes, skimming off any particles that form on top. Carefully pour the butter into a storage container or divide into small portions (an ice cube tray is an ideal container), discarding the watery residue at the bottom. Store the clarified butter covered and refrigerated for up to 1 week or tightly sealed and frozen for up to 3 months.

Crème Fraîche

Although not quite the real thing, good homemade crème fraîche can be made by whisking 1 cup room-temperature cream into 1 cup scalded (heated to just below a boil) whole milk. Cover the mixture and place it in a larger container of warm water. Allow it to rest in a warm (about 110°F) spot (if you have a pilot light in your oven, it should create just enough heat) for about 12 hours, or until very thick and slightly sweet. Cover and refrigerate for up to 1 week.

Bread

Most breads freeze very well. Being a family of six, we usually eat at one sitting even the largest loaf of Italian or French bread that I can buy. I try to keep a loaf or two in the freezer for last-minute warming in the oven if I haven't had time to stop at one of the superb artisanal bakeries that we have in New York. Many supermarkets now have their own bakeries, where you can buy quite a variety of freshly baked breads.

I sometimes even make a loaf or two of garlic bread to keep in the freezer. All you need to do is chop a head of garlic and mix it into about $1/2$ cup of olive oil (this is particularly easy to do in a small food processor). Slice the loaf lengthwise in half and, using a pastry brush, generously coat the cut sides with the garlic-flavored oil. Place the top of the loaf back on the bottom and tightly wrap in plastic wrap. Label and freeze. To serve, unwrap and bake in a preheated 350°F oven for about 20 minutes. If desired, sprinkle with a bit of freshly grated Parmesan or Romano cheese before baking.

A Group of Soups

In my restaurants, soups are often the delicate introduction to a rich, luxurious meal, but at home they are more frequently the meal itself. Served with some warm, crusty bread, a mixed green salad (often made with crisp bitter greens), and a glass of wine or a frosty cold beer (fresh lemonade or chocolate milk for the kids), most of the soups that I make at home meet the requirements for a filling lunch or a light supper. All of the boys, including our three-year-old twins, Eric and Reed, can be counted on to make a beeline for a bowl of homemade soup. Their favorite remains my Mom's Chicken Noodle Soup, which always seems to make them feel better when they are hit with the inevitable winter cold.

The great thing about putting a soup together is that you can often use bits and pieces of leftovers. Never throw away a poultry carcass or meat bones—you will be amazed at how much flavor these can add to a simple vegetable soup made with carrots, potatoes, onions, or leeks (which we all usually have on hand), and any other vegetables you might find in the fridge. Plus, even when you're following a recipe, if you don't have a particular ingredient on hand, ready substitutions of different herbs or vegetables will usually only enhance the end result.

In this chapter, I've put together a group of soups that run the gamut from a light and low-cal Fresh Snap Pea Soup to an almost-classic French onion soup to a hearty main-course Fish Soup with Rouille and Parmesan Toasts. Each soup can stand on its own as a simple meal, be served as a first course for a dinner party, or be paired with sandwiches for casual weekend entertaining.

Charlie's Famous Corn Chowder

Cooking the corncobs with the milk and broth infuses the chowder liquid with an intense corn flavor, a no-longer-secret technique that gives this soup the name "Charlie's Famous." To add a little heat to the soup, sauté some chopped chile peppers and garlic with the leeks and bell pepper. For a very hearty main-course soup, add chunks of white fish such as monkfish or halibut with the corn kernels. Any leftover chowder can be pureed and served cold with some plain yogurt stirred into it.

SERVES 6

10 ears corn, shucked

6 cups milk

2 cups chicken broth

3/4 pound slab bacon, cut into 1/4-inch dice

1 cup chopped leeks (white and some of the green part)

1/2 cup diced red bell pepper

3 medium potatoes, peeled and cut into 1/4-inch dice

Coarse salt and freshly ground black pepper

2 tablespoons chopped fresh chives

1. Using a chef's knife and cutting close to the cob, slice the kernels from the corncobs. Set the kernels aside.

2. Combine the cobs with the milk and broth in a large pot over medium heat. Bring to a boil, then immediately lower the heat and simmer for 15 minutes. Remove the pot from the heat. Using tongs, remove the cobs from the hot liquid and allow them to stand until cool enough to handle. Set the pot aside.

Holding the cooled cobs upright in a shallow dish, carefully scrape all of the residue from them with a knife. Add these corn scrapings to the pot and discard the cobs.

3. While the liquid is being infused with the corn, fry the bacon in a large sauté pan over medium-low heat, stirring frequently, for 10 to 15 minutes, or until all of its fat has been rendered. Using a slotted spoon, lift the bacon pieces from the pan and place them on a double layer of paper towels to drain.

4. Pour off most of the fat from the pan, leaving about 1 tablespoon. Return the pan to medium heat and add the leeks and bell pepper. Sauté for about 7 minutes, or until the vegetables are just softened. Using a slotted spoon, transfer the vegetables to the milk mixture, first allowing the excess fat to drain off through the spoon.

5. Place the pot over medium heat. Add the potatoes and season to taste with salt and pepper. Bring to a boil, then lower the heat and simmer for about 20 minutes, or until the potatoes are tender. Add the reserved corn kernels, bring to a simmer, and simmer for 5 minutes.

6. Remove about 2 cups of the chowder and puree it until smooth in a blender or food processor. Return the puree to the chowder and simmer for an additional 5 minutes. Stir in the chives and the reserved bacon. Taste and, if necessary, adjust the seasoning with salt and pepper and serve.

Summer Vegetable Minestrone with Pesto

Traditionally minestrone is a thick, hearty winter vegetable soup that contains lots of root vegetables, pasta, and, often, dried beans or peas. I have taken the idea and turned minestrone into a *minestrina*, or little soup, a thin brothy soup with just barely cooked vegetables and fresh beans and no pasta. I add a taste of garlicky pesto for a little extra zest. Although pesto is traditionally made from basil, you can vary the flavor by changing the herb, as suggested in the recipe. You can also add some sun-dried tomatoes, roasted garlic, or orange zest for a slight change of pace.

SERVES 6

3 large (about 1 pound) ripe tomatoes

8 cups homemade or canned vegetable broth (see page 6)

Coarse salt and freshly ground black pepper

1 cup shelled fresh cranberry beans

½ cup finely diced carrots

¼ cup finely diced sweet onion (such as Vidalia)

½ cup finely diced yellow squash

½ cup finely diced zucchini

½ cup fresh peas

½ cup fresh corn kernels

Pesto (recipe follows)

1. Peel, core, seed, and chop the tomatoes. Place them in a food processor and process to a very smooth puree.

2. Combine the tomato puree, vegetable broth, and salt and pepper to taste in a large saucepan over medium heat. Stir in the cranberry beans, carrots, and onion. Bring to a simmer and simmer for 10 minutes. Stir in the yellow squash, zucchini, peas, and corn and cook for about 10 minutes longer; the vegetables should remain a bit crisp. Taste and, if necessary, adjust the seasoning with salt and pepper. Remove from the heat and serve with a dollop of pesto in the center of each bowl.

Pesto

MAKES ABOUT 1½ CUPS

2 cups loosely packed fresh basil, cilantro, mint, or parsley leaves
½ cup chopped pine nuts or hazelnuts (see Note)
6 cloves garlic, chopped
½ cup freshly grated Parmesan cheese
½ to ¾ cup extra virgin olive oil
Coarse salt and freshly ground black pepper

Combine the basil, nuts, garlic, and cheese in the bowl of a food processor and process until the mixture is thick and pastelike. With the machine running, slowly add enough of the olive oil to make a smooth, thick sauce. Season to taste with salt and pepper. Use immediately, or store, tightly covered and refrigerated, for up to 1 week. If you are planning to freeze the pesto, do not add the nuts or cheese, as once frozen, they will give the sauce an unappetizing texture. May be frozen for up to 2 months. Once thawed, puree with nuts and cheese.

NOTE: Toast the nuts for a richer flavor in the finished pesto.

The Best Butternut Squash Soup

A version of this soup first appeared in my cookbook *Great American Food*. When doing a cooking demonstration to promote the book, I often prepared this soup because it was quick and easy to do. It remains one of my favorites, and I keep tinkering with it. Here's my newest variation.

SERVES 6

3 large butternut squash (see Note)

1 cup chopped shallots

Approximately ¾ cup honey

2 tablespoons minced fresh savory

¼ teaspoon ground nutmeg

¼ teaspoon ground cinnamon

¼ teaspoon ground ginger

¼ teaspoon ground cardamom

4½ cups chicken broth, heated

Coarse salt and freshly ground black pepper

Approximately ⅓ cup plain yogurt

2 tablespoons minced fresh chives or flat-leaf parsley

1. Peel, halve, and seed the squash. Cut it into ¾-inch dice. Combine the squash with the shallots in a steamer basket over boiling water. Steam for 12 minutes, or until the squash is tender.

2. Working in 2 batches, place half the squash and half the shallots in the bowl of a food processor, add about a quarter of

the honey, half of the savory, nutmeg, cinnamon, ginger, and cardamom, and begin processing; with the motor running, pour in half of the broth and process until very smooth. Repeat with a second batch.

3. Pour the soup into a medium saucepan and season to taste with salt and pepper and, if necessary, all or part of the remaining honey. (The amount of honey required will vary depending on the sweetness of the squash.)

4. Place the saucepan over medium heat and bring to a simmer. Simmer for 5 minutes. Serve hot, garnished with a dollop of yogurt and minced chives.

Creamy Potato Soup

When I was a child, potato soup was one of my mom's favorite stick-to-your-ribs lunches. She used a heavy hand with the cream and butter, which made the soup so deliciously warming on a freezing, snowy day. Mom's soup was thick and chunky, not vichyssoise-smooth. I've cut down—just a bit—on the butter and cream, but my big boys, Court and Randall, still think that this potato soup is just about the best thing since Barney. Weekend guests, once they've feasted on a bowl, always ask for a take-home container.

SERVES 6

½ pound slab bacon, cut into small cubes

3 tablespoons unsalted butter

6 leeks (white part only), well washed and sliced crosswise into chunks

2½ pounds all-purpose potatoes, peeled and cubed

5 cups chicken broth

3 cups half-and-half

1 cup heavy cream

Coarse salt and freshly ground white pepper

2 tablespoons chopped fresh dill

1. Place the bacon in a large frying pan over low heat. Fry, stirring frequently, for about 15 minutes, or until the bacon is crisp and has rendered all of its fat. (If this is happening more quickly, turn down the heat so that you do not shrink the bacon too much.) Using a slotted spoon, lift

the bacon from the pan and set aside on a double layer of paper towels to drain.

2. Melt the butter in a large soup pot over medium heat. Add the leeks and cook, stirring frequently, for about 8 minutes, or until the leeks are quite soft but not taking on any color.

3. Stir in the potatoes. Add the broth and half-and-half and bring to a boil. Lower the heat and simmer for 15 minutes, or until the potatoes are almost tender.

4. Add the cream and salt and pepper to taste and cook for an additional 10 minutes. Taste and, if necessary, adjust the seasoning with salt and pepper. Stir in the dill and the reserved bacon and serve.

Onion Soup in the French Tradition

When I think of onion soup, I am immediately transported to Paris and images of smocked workers inhaling steaming bowls of soup in the early morning light. Fanciful dreaming, perhaps, but it nonetheless urges me into the kitchen to re-create the sights and aromas of the Paris markets. The deep flavor of the slowly caramelized nontraditional red onions adds richness and strong resonant color to this very simple soup. Perfect when perching in front of a football game on television on a cold winter weekend.

SERVES 6

2 leeks (white and some of the green part), split lengthwise, well washed, and thinly sliced

4 tablespoons (½ stick) unsalted butter

5 medium red onions, thinly sliced

1 cup thinly sliced shallots

2 tablespoons balsamic vinegar

⅛ teaspoon dried thyme

1 cup dry red wine

5 cups chicken broth

4 cups beef broth

Coarse salt and freshly ground black pepper

6 large or 12 small slices French baguette, toasted

½ cup grated Gruyère cheese

1. Trim off the root end and most of the green from the leeks. Cut them lengthwise in half and wash well under cold running water; leeks have a lot of sand. Pat dry and cut them crosswise into thin slices. Set aside.

2. Melt the butter in a large soup pot over medium heat. Add the onions, shallots, and leeks and cook, stirring frequently, for about 12 minutes, or until the vegetables are beginning to take on some color. Immediately lower the heat and continue to cook, stirring frequently, for about 30 minutes, or until the onion mixture is richly colored, almost a deep brown color. Throughout the cooking process, watch carefully, as you do not want any burning to occur.

3. Stir in the balsamic vinegar and thyme and cook for 3 minutes. Add the red wine, raise the heat, and bring to a simmer. Simmer for about 10 minutes, or until some of the wine has cooked off. Add the broths and season to taste with salt and pepper. Bring to a simmer, then lower the heat and cook for about 20 minutes, or until the soup has developed a rich brown color and is very aromatic. You may want to cover the soup for the last half of the cooking to prevent more of the liquid from evaporating.

4. When ready to serve, preheat the broiler.

5. Transfer the soup to deep heatproof soup bowls or crocks. Place the toasts on top of the soup and sprinkle with the cheese. Place under the broiler for 2 minutes, or until the cheese is beginning to bubble and turn golden brown. Serve immediately. To prevent burned lips, make sure that the kids' servings are allowed to cool a bit.

Mushroom Soup (without Cream)

In central New York State, where I grew up, spring brings with it a bounty of morels and leeks. The many abandoned apple orchards create the perfect home for the cap-shaped earthy fungus to flourish, and acres of damp woodlands are redolent with the pungent scent of wild leeks, also called ramps. It is a food lover's springtime paradise, and this soup uses these gifts of the earth to their best advantage.

SERVES 6

2 pounds wild mushrooms—if possible, a mix of morels and one or two others (see Note)

2 tablespoons canola oil

1/2 cup chopped leeks (white part only) (see Note)

1 celery stalk, peeled and minced

1/2 teaspoon minced fresh thyme

2 tablespoons dry sherry

3 cups chicken broth

2 cups beef broth

Coarse salt and freshly ground black pepper

3 cups pureed white beans (about two 16-ounce cans) (see Note)

Ground nutmeg

1. Using a soft brush or a clean towel, carefully clean the mushrooms of all debris. Remove any tough stems and roughly slice the mushrooms: You want a rustic look, so don't try to create perfect slices. Set aside.

2. Heat the oil in a large soup pot over medium heat. Add the leeks and celery and sauté for about 5 minutes, or until the vegetables are quite soft but not brown. Stir in the thyme and sherry and cook for 3 minutes. Add the mushrooms and sauté for an additional 5 minutes.

3. Add the broths and season to taste with salt and pepper. Raise the heat and bring to a boil, then lower the heat and cook for 20 minutes, or until the mushrooms are very tender and the broth is infused with their flavor.

4. Stir the bean puree into the soup. Season to taste with nutmeg and, if necessary, additional salt and pepper. Cook for 5 minutes, or until the soup is well blended and very hot. Serve immediately or cool (preferably in an ice-water bath), cover, and refrigerate for up to 3 days.

NOTE: If you can't buy wild mushrooms, use an equal amount of button mushrooms. However, add ½ cup dried mushrooms (morels, porcini, or shiitake) that have been soaked in 1 cup of hot water for 30 minutes. Chop the softened dried mushrooms; strain the soaking water through cheesecloth and add both to the soup to enrich the stock.

   If you can find them, use wild leeks (or ramps) in place of the leeks; they have an unforgettable pungent flavor.

   Canned white beans that have been rinsed, such as cannellini or small white beans, can be used.

Fresh Snap Pea Soup

Is there anything sweeter than a just-picked pea-filled pod? It's difficult for me to pick enough peas for a meal from my garden because I eat two or three for every pod I pick. So, don't hesitate to make this soup if you, like me, have to rely on frozen peas or a combination of frozen and fresh. I love the taste of this soup so much that I have often had to purchase those little plastic-wrapped packages of sugar snap peas (found in many supermarket produce sections) to supplement my harvest.

SERVES 6

5 cups canned vegetable broth (see page 6)

1 pound sugar snap peas, tough ends trimmed

¼ cup chopped scallions

¼ cup chopped celery

1 teaspoon minced fresh oregano

Coarse salt and freshly ground white pepper

1 cup plain nonfat yogurt, at room temperature

1 tablespoon chopped fresh dill

1. Place the vegetable broth in a large saucepan over medium-high heat and bring to a boil. Add the snap peas, scallions, celery, oregano, and salt and pepper to taste. Return to a boil, then immediately lower the heat and simmer for 10 minutes.

2. Carefully pour the soup into a blender (this may have to be done in batches) or food processor and process until smooth. Return to a clean saucepan and place over medium heat. Heat, stirring frequently, for about 3 minutes, or until the

soup is very hot. Remove from the heat and stir in the yogurt and dill. Serve immediately.

3. For a chilled soup, pour the pureed soup into a bowl or other container and place in a larger container of ice and water to cool quickly. Stir occasionally. When cool, cover and refrigerate for about 3 hours, or until very well chilled. (The soup can be refrigerated for up to 3 days.) Just before serving, whisk in the yogurt and dill.

Easy Gazpacho

This gazpacho is one of my favorite summertime soups. It is easy to make in large batches, requires no cooking, and is packed with flavor. I don't like much heat in my cooking, but if you do, add some minced jalapeño or serrano chiles to taste for that extra bite.

If you have leftover gazpacho, puree it, heat it up a bit (stir in a tablespoon of butter for richness), and use it as a sauce for grilled poultry, fish, or pork.

SERVES 6

3 cups tomato juice

½ cup red wine vinegar

2 tablespoons extra virgin olive oil

2 pounds very ripe tomatoes, peeled, cored, seeded, and finely diced

1 large cucumber, peeled, seeded, and finely diced

1 large red bell pepper, cored, seeded, and finely diced

1 large red onion, finely diced

1 tablespoon minced garlic or Roasted Garlic (page 6)

Coarse salt and freshly ground black pepper

¼ cup finely chopped fresh flat-leaf parsley, cilantro, or chives

1. Combine the tomato juice, vinegar, and olive oil in a large bowl. Add the tomatoes, cucumber, bell pepper, onion, and garlic. Season to taste with salt and pepper. Cover and refrigerate for about 2 hours, or until nicely chilled.

2. Stir in the chopped herbs and serve cold.

NOTE: For speed, chop the vegetables in a food processor, but take care not to overprocess them. I prefer to take the time to hand-dice the vegetables, as they look more attractive in the finished soup. If you do hand-dice, make sure to catch the juices and add them to the soup.

If you want a gussied-up gazpacho, add a few cooked shrimp or some cooked lobster or crabmeat to each bowl just before serving.

Fish Soup with Rouille and Parmesan Toasts

The more fishing I do, the more fish soups I make. On weekends, I try to get out on Long Island Sound, where I can hook some bass for an evening's meal. This soup, which I often make with my catch, is quite similar to the classic French bouillabaisse, but it lacks the hint of expensive saffron and the jolt of Pernod offered by the original. If you are looking for real French flavor, don't hesitate to add those traditional flavors (about ¹/₂ teaspoon saffron threads and a tablespoon or two of Pernod) to this base.

If you can't buy bass, snapper, or halibut, use whatever type of fish you can get locally. In a pinch, you can even use frozen. A rich, full-flavored broth such as this allows you a little more leeway than a recipe where the flavor of the fish is predominant. The Rouille and Parmesan Toasts make a great garnish, but they are not absolutely essential.

SERVES 6

3 tablespoons olive oil

2 leeks (white and some of the green part), well-washed, split lengthwise, and chopped

¹/₂ cup chopped celery

1 tablespoon chopped garlic

1 fennel bulb, trimmed and finely diced, optional

1 cup dry white wine

2 tablespoons chopped sun-dried tomato

1 medium orange (not peeled), quartered and seeded

1 bay leaf

¹/₂ teaspoon dried thyme

¹/₂ teaspoon red pepper flakes, or to taste

3 cups chopped canned Italian plum tomatoes, with their juice

2 cups clam juice

Coarse salt

12 clams, well scrubbed (see Note)

12 mussels, well scrubbed and debearded (see Note)

1 pound skinless, boneless bass, snapper, halibut, or any firm-fleshed white fish, or a
    combination, cut into chunks

1/2 pound small shrimp, peeled and deveined

Rouille (recipe follows), optional

Parmesan Toasts (recipe follows), optional

1. Heat the oil in a large soup pot over medium heat. Add the leeks, celery, and garlic and sauté for about 5 minutes, or until the vegetables have softened slightly. If using the fennel, add it and sauté for an additional 3 minutes.

2. Add the wine, raise the heat, and bring to a boil. Boil for 5 minutes. Stir in the sun-dried tomato and boil for 1 additional minute. Stir in the orange, bay leaf, thyme, and red pepper flakes. Then add the tomatoes and clam juice and bring to a boil. Immediately lower the heat and simmer for 20 minutes. Season to taste with salt.

3. Add the clams and mussels and cook, stirring frequently, for about 5 minutes, or until the shellfish begin to open. Stir in the fish chunks and cook for 3 minutes. Stir in the shrimp and cook for an additional 3 minutes, or until all of the seafood is just cooked. Remove and discard the orange, bay leaf, and any clams and mussels that have not opened.

4. Serve in shallow soup bowls with a dollop of rouille in the center and 2 Parmesan toasts on the side of each, if desired.

NOTE: You can use all clams or all mussels if you're short on one or have a lot of the other.

Rouille

MAKES ABOUT 1 CUP

A very simple version of the homemade garlic mayonnaise that is the traditional French accompaniment to bouillabaisse.

3/4 cup fine-quality mayonnaise

1/4 cup fine bread crumbs

2 tablespoons chopped jarred or canned roasted Italian red bell peppers packed in oil

2 cloves garlic

Coarse salt

1/8 teaspoon cayenne pepper, or to taste

Place the mayonnaise in the bowl of a small food processor or a blender, add the bread crumbs, bell peppers, and garlic, and process to a thick puree. Season to taste with salt and the cayenne. Scrape the rouille into a nonreactive container, cover, and refrigerate until ready to use. May be kept, covered and refrigerated, for up to 3 days.

Parmesan Toasts

MAKES 12

Twelve ½-inch-thick slices French bread cut on the diagonal
1 large clove garlic, halved
¾ cup freshly grated Parmesan cheese
1 tablespoon minced fresh flat-leaf parsley

1. Preheat the oven to 375°F. Line a baking sheet with parchment paper.

2. Lay the bread out on the baking sheet. Using the cut sides, rub one side of each slice of bread with the garlic.

3. Combine the cheese with the parsley. Sprinkle an equal portion of the cheese mixture on each slice of bread. Bake for about 10 minutes, or until the cheese is melted and golden and the bread is toasted.

NOTE: The toasts can be made early in the day and stored, uncovered, at room temperature. Or make them a few days in advance and store them tightly sealed at room temperature. If they become a bit soggy, reheat them to crisp just before serving.

Saffron-Mussel Soup with Fennel

This soup is more main course than appetizer. Serve it with piles of warm, crusty bread so that every drop of the rich broth can be eaten. The richness of this soup calls for a salad of bitter greens (and perhaps some orange sections) to balance the intense flavor. Then, of course, you have to have a glass of crisp white wine. So, there you go, dinner.

SERVES 6

2 fennel bulbs

Coarse salt

6 pounds mussels, well scrubbed and debearded

3 cups dry white wine

5 shallots, chopped

2 cloves garlic, chopped

1 tablespoon minced fresh flat-leaf parsley

1 teaspoon minced fresh thyme

1 teaspoon minced fresh chervil

⅛ teaspoon saffron threads

3 cups half-and-half

1 cup heavy cream

Freshly ground white pepper

1. Trim the fennel bulbs, reserving the fronds. Cut the fennel bulbs into ¼-inch dice. Chop enough of the fronds to make ½ cup and mince enough of them to make 2 tablespoons. Reserve the chopped and minced fronds separately.

2. Place the diced fennel in a medium saucepan with cold water to cover, add salt to taste, and bring to a boil over high heat. Lower the heat and simmer for about 4 minutes, or until the fennel is crisp-tender. Drain well and pat dry. Set aside.

3. Discard any mussels that have cracked or otherwise damaged shells. Remove the beards (the hairy outgrowth attached to the shell) from the mussels. Using a brush, scrub each mussel under cold running water. Then rinse the mussels in a sink or large bowl of cold water to cover until the water remains clear; this may require several rinses, as you want to remove as much of the grit as possible.

4. Place the mussels in a large soup pot, and the wine, shallots, garlic, parsley, thyme, chervil, saffron, and the reserved chopped fennel fronds, cover, and bring to a boil over high heat. Boil, occasionally stirring up the mussels, for about 10 minutes, or until the mussels have opened. Remove from the heat and, using a slotted spoon, lift the mussels from the cooking liquid; discard any mussels that have not opened. Set the mussels aside to cool.

5. Strain the mussel cooking liquid through a very fine sieve lined with multiple layers of slightly damp cheesecloth (or paper towels) into a clean saucepan; you want to ensure that no grit remains in the liquid. Set aside.

6. As soon as the mussels are cool enough to handle, remove them from their shells, discarding the shells. Set aside.

7. Add the half-and-half and cream to the mussel cooking liquid, place the pan over medium heat, season to taste with salt and pepper, and bring to a simmer. Simmer for about 7 minutes, or until slightly thickened. Add the mussels and the reserved diced fennel and simmer for 5 minutes. Serve hot, garnished with the reserved minced fennel fronds.

Mom's Chicken Noodle Soup

This is one soup that can't be made without using the real thing—a good rich chicken stock. Stock is, however, easy and inexpensive to make with the leftover carcass of a Perfect Roast Chicken. As soon as dinner is finished, toss the carcass of the roast chicken into a pot with vegetables and water and get the stock going while cleaning up the kitchen. If you don't have a carcass, buy some chicken parts (wings, necks, and backs are best if you can find them) and start from scratch. The aroma from the simmering stock is almost as curative as the soup itself.

SERVES 6 TO 8

Chicken Stock

1 or 2 carcasses from Perfect Roast Chicken (page 138), chopped into pieces (see Note), or 4 pounds chicken parts

1 large carrot, peeled and chopped

1 large onion, chopped

1 celery stalk, chopped

About 10 parsley stems with some leaves

10 peppercorns

2 bay leaves

½ teaspoon dried thyme

Coarse salt

½ pound fine egg noodles

1 cup finely diced carrots

1 cup finely diced celery

1 cup frozen petit peas, thawed

1 tablespoon minced fresh flat-leaf parsley

Coarse salt and freshly ground black pepper

1. To make the stock, you can simply throw the carcass(es), along with the chopped carrot, onion, and celery, into a large deep soup pot or stockpot with cold water to cover by about 1 inch. But if you'd like a deeper-colored, richer-tasting stock, first place the carcasses or parts in a roasting pan in a preheated 400°F oven and roast for about 20 minutes (for the carcasses) or 1 hour (for the parts), until nicely browned, then combine them with the chopped vegetables in the pot with water to cover by 1 inch.

2. Bring the water to a boil, then add the parsley stems, peppercorns, bay leaves, thyme, and salt to taste. Lower the heat and simmer, skimming off any impurities that rise to the top, for about 2 hours, or until a rich stock has formed. You will, from time to time, have to add water to keep the chicken covered. Strain through a fine sieve into a clean large saucepan. Discard the solids. Skim off the fat (see Note). The stock can be made ahead and refrigerated.

3. Place the stock over high heat and bring to a boil. Add the noodles, diced carrots, and diced celery and simmer for about 6 minutes, or until the noodles are just about tender. Add the peas and simmer for an additional 2 minutes, or until the noodles are very tender. Stir in the minced parsley. Taste and adjust the seasoning with salt and pepper. Serve piping hot.

NOTE: If the carcasses are picked clean of meat, add 4 to 6 chicken wings to the pot for extra flavor.

Chill the stock in an ice-water bath after straining so that the fat will rise to the top and can then be easily skimmed off.

This is the most basic tummy-warming, flu-chasing chicken soup. Feel free to change the herbs, add other diced vegetables or diced chicken breast, throw in a couple of cups of shredded spinach, and/or replace the egg noodles with rice noodles, rice, barley, tortellini, or tiny ravioli—it's your call. To make a one-dish meal, poach 6 to 8 skinless, boneless chicken breast halves in the soup for about 12 minutes and place one in the middle of each dish.

Turkey Soup with Wild Rice

When I was a child, turkeys were only available at the market at holiday time. If it had been a good fall hunting season, wild turkey could be found in my mom's freezer. Nowadays, you can buy whole turkeys and parts, as well as cutlets, all through the year, so this soup doesn't have to be a holiday afterthought. Although most of the recipes in this book rely on canned broths, for this soup you do have to make a stock, preferably from the carcass of a freshly roasted turkey. However, if you don't have a leftover carcass, you can buy turkey wings and/or legs (see Note) to make the soup base.

SERVES 6 TO 8

Turkey Stock

1 large turkey carcass with some meat, chopped into pieces

1 cup dry white wine

2 large carrots, chopped

2 large leeks, trimmed, well washed, and chopped

1 celery stalk, chopped

½ cup dried mushrooms (such as porcini or shiitake)

¼ cup chopped fresh flat-leaf parsley

1 tablespoon peppercorns

3 sprigs fresh thyme

1 bay leaf

Coarse salt

½ cup finely diced carrots

½ cup finely diced parsnips

¼ cup finely diced celery root

1 tablespoon olive oil or unsalted butter

1 tablespoon minced shallots

2 cups sliced wild (or button) mushrooms

½ pound smoked turkey, cut into julienne

3 cups cooked (about 1 pound raw) wild rice

Coarse salt and freshly ground black pepper to taste

1 to 2 teaspoons fresh thyme leaves

1. For the stock, place the carcass in a large soup pot or stockpot. Add the wine, carrots, leeks, celery, dried mushrooms, parsley, peppercorns, thyme sprigs, and bay leaf. Pour in enough cold water to cover the ingredients by 2 inches. Place the pot over high heat and bring to a boil. Season to taste with salt. Lower the heat and simmer, from time to time skimming off the foam and bits that rise to the top with a metal spoon, for 2½ hours, adding water as necessary to keep the carcass and vegetables covered. Strain the liquid through a very fine sieve into a heatproof container, discarding the solids. Place in a larger container of ice and water and allow the stock to cool slightly, stirring from time to time. (The stock can be made up to 3 days in advance, covered, and refrigerated. Or make well in advance and freeze; thaw before using.)

2. One at a time, blanch the diced carrots, parsnips, and celery root in boiling salted water for 1 to 2 minutes, until the color is set and the vegetables are crisp-tender. Remove with a strainer or skimmer, refresh under cold running water, and drain well. Pat dry and reserve.

3. Heat the oil in a large sauté pan over medium heat. Add the shallots and sauté for 3 minutes. Stir in the sliced mushrooms and continue sautéing for about 10 minutes, or until the mushrooms have exuded most of their liquid. Set aside.

4. Place the turkey stock in a large saucepot over medium heat. Add the smoked turkey, wild rice, and the reserved mushroom mixture and bring to a simmer. Simmer for 5 minutes. Stir in the reserved blanched vegetables and simmer for 1

minute. Taste and adjust the seasoning with salt and pepper. Serve hot, with a sprinkling of fresh thyme leaves over the top.

NOTE: When using turkey parts for the stock, roast them for 1 hour in a 400°F oven prior to putting them into the liquid for a deeper, richer flavor. Once used for stock, the meat is not really very tasty, as most of the flavor—and nutrients— have been boiled out. However, in a pinch, you could use it for Turkey Hash (page 149).

All Kinds of Salads

In our house, salads are always a home run. During the summer, our meals can be as simple as one Great Big Salad served by the pool. With so many ingredients, everyone at the table can find something in the bowl that they will like. There is always a basket of bread on the table, so if a sandwich is more appealing, particularly for Eric and Reed, our little guys, we can take some meat, eggs or cheese, and greens from the bowl and fold them into the bread.

Many other salads I've included also serve as great main courses—some of them can even be the main-course feature when entertaining, especially in the warmer months. I often make four or five salads to serve for a casual lunch or supper. I usually prepare several with meat, fish, or cheese and a couple of others that are composed mainly of vegetables. Add a big basket of freshly baked rolls or artisanal breads and a bowl of creamery butter, and even the heartiest appetite will find satisfaction. And, because it has been a meal of salads, everyone will feel extremely virtuous, so you can end your dinner with a lusciously rich dessert.

If it's not a main course you are looking for, you will find a few salads that will serve as an introduction to a dinner party menu as well as those that are traditional side dishes, such as my favorite, Potato Salad, and a really retro Waldorf Salad. Whether you need a complete meal or to complete a meal, I can guarantee that you will find a salad that fits the bill.

One Great Big Salad

The perfect tossed salad is not iceberg lettuce, flavorless tomatoes, and commercially bottled dressing. It is a subtle blend of soft and crisp lettuces mixed with sweet and bitter greens tossed with a nicely balanced homemade vinaigrette. In season, add ripe tomatoes and a variety of fresh raw or lightly blanched vegetables if you like.

Among the salad greens now available are red or green leaf lettuce, Boston, romaine and butter lettuces, mâche (or lamb's tongue), frisée (chicory), arugula, endive, watercress, fennel, radicchio, field greens, spinach, and bok choy and other cabbages, as well as all types of bitter greens. Almost every market, large or small, now sells mixed lettuces and wild greens, known by their French name, mesclun. You can even throw in some edible flowers for color and fragrance.

A basic homemade vinaigrette is three to four parts oil (peanut, olive, or other vegetable oil or a combination, often with a small amount of walnut, sesame, or other intensely flavored oil) to one part acid (wine, champagne, balsamic or fruit-flavored vinegars, or citrus juice), seasoned with salt and pepper. To this basic vinaigrette you might also add Dijon mustard (no more than 2 teaspoons per cup of dressing) and/or minced fresh herbs.

This is the Palmer One Great Big Salad that is as often as not the main course for a meal on a hot summer evening. Use whatever greens are the freshest and crispest or whatever vegetables please your family. Gather lots of leafy greens and crisp vegetables and then accent them with eggs, meat, and/or cheese. If we make too much, I simply throw the remains in a saucepan, add a cup (or less, depending on how much leftover salad I have) of water, cook it for 5 minutes, and then puree the now-soup in a blender. I stir some unflavored yogurt into the puree and chill it for a light cold lunch.

4 cups ½-inch cubes Italian bread

¼ cup olive oil

12 cups chopped, shredded, or pulled-apart mixed greens

4 very ripe tomatoes, peeled, cored, and cut into wedges or thin slices

1 large red onion, sliced

2 beets, peeled and shredded

2 carrots, peeled and shredded

2 ripe avocados, peeled, pitted, and cubed

1 large cucumber, peeled and thinly sliced

½ cup sliced red radishes

1 cup Italian, French, and/or Greek olives, pitted

6 large hard-boiled eggs, peeled and coarsely chopped

1 pound cooked diced chicken, ham, bacon, or roast beef or cubed cheese, such as
    Swiss, cheddar, or goat, optional

Whatever vinaigrette you choose (see headnote)

1. Preheat the oven to 350°F.

2. Toss the bread cubes with the olive oil in a large bowl. Place them on a baking sheet and bake, turning occasionally, for 15 minutes, or until the bread is nicely toasted. Remove from the oven and set aside to cool.

3. Place the greens in a large salad bowl. Add the tomatoes, red onion, beets, carrots, avocados, cucumber, radishes, olives, and croutons. Using your hands, toss to combine the ingredients well. Add the chopped eggs and, if using, the meat or cheese.

4. Pour about ¾ cup of vinaigrette over the top and, using your hands, toss to combine. Serve immediately.

Potato Salad

I'm almost reluctant to write a recipe for potato salad. I have had so many versions—French, German, Southwestern, Greek, deli-style—but I've never really liked any of them as much as I love my mother's old-fashioned American mayonnaise-dressed version. It is what I now usually make for family picnics, cookouts, and summer weekend meals. If you want to add your own flourish, this basic salad might welcome some pickle relish, olives, or roasted red peppers or pimientos. If you are counting calories, you can lighten the dressing by using half nonfat yogurt and half mayonnaise.

SERVES 6 TO 8

8 large all-purpose potatoes, scrubbed

4 large hard-boiled eggs, peeled and chopped

1 cup finely diced celery

½ cup chopped scallions

½ cup finely diced onion

½ teaspoon celery seeds

¼ teaspoon dry mustard

1½ to 2 cups mayonnaise, or to taste

2 tablespoons white vinegar

Coarse salt and freshly ground black pepper

1. Place the potatoes in a large saucepan with cold water to cover and bring to a boil over medium-high heat. Boil for about 30 minutes, or until the potatoes are tender when pierced with the point of a small sharp knife. Drain well and allow to cool slightly.

2. When the potatoes are cool enough to handle, peel and cut them into 1- to 1½-inch chunks. Place the potatoes in a large bowl. Add the eggs, celery, scallions, and onion and toss to combine.

3. Stir the celery seeds and mustard into 1 cup of the mayonnaise. Add the vinegar and stir to blend well. Fold the mayonnaise into the potato mixture, taking care not to mash the potatoes. Season to taste with salt and pepper, and add additional mayonnaise until the salad is as moist as you like. Cover and refrigerate for at least 2 hours before serving.

NOTE: If you have the courage to handle the potatoes when they are still quite hot, cut and dress them with the mayonnaise. They will absorb much more of the dressing, and the salad will be more deeply flavored. Do not add the eggs, celery, scallions, and onion until the potatoes have cooled slightly.

Roasted Wild Mushroom Salad

Unless you live in an area where they are commonly available in spring, morels are a luxury item. If you can find them, their intense smoky flavor is the perfect match for peppery dandelion greens. Don't hesitate to make this salad with whatever mushrooms and greens are in season.

SERVES 6

1 pound morels or other wild mushrooms (see Note)

⅓ cup extra virgin olive oil

1 tablespoon minced garlic

Coarse salt and freshly ground black pepper to taste

½ cup dry white wine

1 pound baby dandelion greens or arugula, trimmed of tough stems, well washed, and dried (see Note)

2 tablespoons toasted pine nuts

1 tablespoon grated orange zest

¼ pound ricotta salata cheese (see Note), optional

1. Using a soft brush or a clean towel, carefully clean the mushrooms of all debris. If using morels and they are very dirty, give them a quick rinse under cool running water and pat them dry. Trim off the stems and any bruised parts.

2. Preheat the oven to 450°F.

3. Heat the oil in a large ovenproof skillet over medium heat. Add the garlic and sauté for 1 minute. Stir in the morels. When they are nicely coated with the garlic and oil, place the pan in the oven. Roast the mushrooms for about 8 minutes, or

until they are beginning to brown. (If you smell the garlic beginning to burn, remove the pan from the oven. Take out any darkened garlic and turn down the heat. When the oven has cooled a bit, return the pan to the oven and continue to cook the mushrooms.)

4. Remove the pan from the oven and immediately add the wine. Place the pan over high heat and bring the wine to a boil. Boil, stirring constantly, for 2 minutes, or until the wine and hot pan juices are emulsified and smooth. Remove from the heat.

5. Place the dandelion greens in a large heatproof bowl. Add the pine nuts and orange zest, then toss in the hot mushroom mixture until well combined. (The heat will cause the greens to wilt slightly.)

6. Place the salad on a serving platter and, if using, shave the cheese with a vegetable peeler over the salad. Serve immediately.

NOTE: If wild mushrooms are not in season, use sliced portobellos, shiitakes, cremini, or even big white mushrooms, all of which are available year-round in the supermarket.

You can replace the dandelion greens with any slightly spicy green—watercress, frisée, escarole, or arugula, as suggested in the ingredients list.

The cheese is just a wonderful finish to this salad. If you can't find ricotta salata, try Parmesan or a hard goat cheese.

Celery Rémoulade

Celery rémoulade is an old-fashioned, traditional French salad or hors d'oeuvre. When I first began to cook professionally, it was on the menu at every French restaurant, but now you rarely see it. The base of the sauce is a homemade mayonnaise, but, for casual cooks, a fine-quality commercial mayonnaise will do just fine. For color, you can add some julienned carrots or red radishes. The rémoulade can be served as is or on a bed of soft lettuce or crispy bitter greens.

SERVES 6

1 cup fine-quality mayonnaise

1 tablespoon Dijon mustard

1 teaspoon anchovy paste

Pinch of curry powder, or to taste

2 hard-boiled egg yolks, mashed

1 tablespoon finely chopped cornichons or sour pickles

1 tablespoon minced fresh flat-leaf parsley

1 teaspoon minced fresh tarragon

½ teaspoon grated orange zest

Coarse salt and freshly ground white pepper

Juice of 1 lemon

2 large celery roots

1. Whisk together the mayonnaise, mustard, anchovy paste, and curry powder in a medium bowl. When well blended, whisk in the mashed egg yolks. Fold in the cornichons, parsley, tarragon, and orange zest. Taste and, if necessary, season

with salt and white pepper. Cover and refrigerate until ready to use. (May be made up to 1 day in advance of use.)

2. Combine the lemon juice with about 4 cups ice water in a large bowl. Peel each celery root and cut it into quarters. Working with a section at a time, cut it into matchstick-sized pieces. Place the matchsticks in the acidulated ice water as they are cut to keep them from discoloring.

3. When all of the celery root has been cut, drain it well and pat dry. If it is not very, very crisp, place it in a bowl, cover, and refrigerate for 30 minutes.

4. Add the celery root to the rémoulade sauce, tossing to coat well. Serve cold.

Watercress with Baked Goat Cheese and Toasted Walnuts

In the early '80s, when American cheese makers began producing fresh goat cheese, a baked goat cheese salad could be found on almost every restaurant menu. Unlike many other recipes-of-the-moment that quickly go by the wayside, though, a warm goat cheese–bitter green salad has remained a favorite. The fragrant creaminess of the warm cheese seems to caress the spiciness of the greens in the perfect marriage of flavor and texture. Add the crunch of toasted nuts, and you have created a matchless meal. Served with a loaf of raisin-walnut bread, this is often our weekend lunch.

SERVES 6

½ cup extra virgin olive oil

1 cup fine bread crumbs

Twelve ½-inch-thick rounds fresh goat cheese, about ½ inch in diameter (about 8 ounces)

3 bunches watercress, tough stems removed and well washed (see Note)

Orange-Walnut Vinaigrette (recipe follows)

1 cup toasted walnut pieces

1. Preheat the oven to 375°F. Line a baking sheet with parchment paper or aluminum foil. Set aside.

2. Place the olive oil and the bread crumbs on two separate plates or shallow bowls.

3. One at a time, dip the cheese rounds into the olive oil and then into the bread crumbs to coat lightly, and place on the

baking sheet, leaving at least 2 inches between each round. Bake for about 5 minutes, or just until the cheese rounds are golden and bubbling slightly but are not melted. Remove from the oven and allow to stand for 1 minute.

4. Meanwhile, toss the watercress with just enough of the vinaigrette to coat it lightly. Divide the watercress among six plates and place 2 goat cheese rounds in the center of each. Drizzle a bit of the vinaigrette over the cheese rounds, sprinkle the walnuts over all, and serve.

Orange-Walnut Vinaigrette

MAKES ABOUT 1 CUP

⅓ cup fresh orange juice (see Note)
¼ cup white wine vinegar
½ tablespoon minced shallots
½ cup grapeseed, canola, or other neutral vegetable oil
¼ cup walnut oil (see Note)
Coarse salt and freshly ground black pepper

Combine the orange juice, vinegar, and shallots in a small jar with a lid. Shake to combine. Add the oils and salt and pepper to taste. Shake well to combine. Taste and adjust the seasoning if necessary. Use immediately or store, covered and refrigerated, for up to 3 days.

NOTE: For an intense orange flavor, place ⅔ cup of orange juice in a small saucepan over high heat and boil until it is reduced by half.

If the suggested amount of walnut oil seems too intense for your taste, start by adding a tablespoon or two of walnut oil and continue adding small amounts until the vinaigrette is to your liking. Balance the amount of oil required with the unflavored oil. Walnut oil is a bit expensive and goes rancid rather quickly. Buy only a small amount and store it, tightly sealed, in the refrigerator.

Composed Salad of Fennel, Oven-Dried Pears, and Maytag Blue Cheese

Oven-drying fruits and vegetables has become one of my passions. It takes time but no real effort, which makes it a perfect technique for casual cooking. Turn the oven on to its lowest setting, add a tray or two of cut-up or sliced fruits or vegetables, and go about your business. Start checking after two hours to see how far along the drying process is. If you want something to be very dry, allow it to sit in a very low oven overnight or all day. Make dried plum tomatoes and then season with a bit of olive oil, a touch of balsamic, and some fresh herbs, or just leave them as is for an aromatic addition to soups or stews.

In our house, drying fruits is the real deal. Home-dried fruits—especially pineapple, peaches, and pears—make great snacks for the kids, easy desserts accompanied by some yogurt, port, or ice cream, or a unique addition to soups, stews, or salads.

SERVES 6

6 Comice pears

1/2 cup packed light brown sugar

1 teaspoon grated fresh ginger

1/2 cup extra virgin olive oil

3 tablespoons balsamic vinegar

Coarse salt and freshly cracked black pepper to taste

2 medium fennel bulbs, trimmed

2 heads red oak leaf lettuce or other soft buttery lettuce, leaves separated, well washed, and dried

½ cup toasted walnut pieces (black walnuts add an interesting touch)

¼ pound Maytag Blue cheese or other blue cheese

1. Preheat the oven to 200°F or its lowest setting. Line a baking sheet with parchment paper. Set aside.

2. Peel the pears. Cut them lengthwise in half and carefully remove the cores and stems.

3. Combine the brown sugar and ginger, mixing well. Generously rub each pear half with the mixture. Lay the coated pears on the prepared baking sheet and place in the oven to dry for about 6 hours, or until the pears are just beginning to dry out but still retain some of their moisture.

4. Whisk together the olive oil and vinegar in a small bowl. Season to taste with salt and cracked pepper. Set aside.

5. Cut the fennel bulbs lengthwise in half, then cut the fennel lengthwise into very thin slices.

6. Beginning at the flower end, cut each pear lengthwise in half but not through the stem end.

7. Toss the lettuce and fennel together in a large bowl. Add a small amount of the dressing and toss to coat. Place the lettuce mixture on a large serving plate. Fan the pear halves across the greens, criss-crossing the stem ends. Sprinkle the walnut pieces around the edge of the platter, crumble the blue cheese over the top, and drizzle the remaining dressing over all. Serve immediately.

Waldorf Salad

When I was growing up, Waldorf salad was always on our holiday table, but it never appeared at any other time of the year. It was one of my favorites, perhaps because it was a rare treat—or maybe it was the miniature marshmallows that my mother added. In my updated version, which I make throughout the fall, there are no marshmallows for the boys to pick out, but it still is one of their favorite salads, served with their sandwich of the moment.

SERVES 6

½ cup fine-quality mayonnaise

¼ cup crème fraîche, store-bought or homemade (see page 8)

1 tablespoon apple cider

1 teaspoon walnut oil

Pinch of curry powder

2 cups diced crisp apples (see Note)

1 cup diced celery root

½ cup halved seedless red grapes

¾ cup toasted walnut pieces

1. Combine the mayonnaise, crème fraîche, cider, walnut oil, and curry powder in a small bowl, whisking to mix well.

2. Toss together the apples, celery root, and grapes in a medium bowl. Add the mayonnaise mixture and toss to combine. Toss with the nuts and serve. Can be made no more than 3 hours ahead. (If not serving immediately, don't add the nuts, as they will soften; add them just before serving.)

NOTE: You might want to use some of the heirloom apples (such as King David, Stayman Winesap, Newton, and Pippin) now available. They are often a bit tart and very crisp. When preparing the apples, sprinkle a bit of lemon juice on them to keep them from discoloring.

Yellow Beet, Snow Pea, and Jícama Salad

Yellow beets are used here simply to keep the usual beet-red color from running and looking messy, but if you don't mind a bit of staining on your salad, use the more readily available red beets. The jícama, which is a crisp, slightly sweet root vegetable used in Mexican cooking and available at most large supermarkets, can be replaced with celery root, or even fennel, if you can't find it. While this presentation is rather fancy, you can, if the urge hits, just toss all of the ingredients together in one big bowl.

SERVES 6

1½ pounds small yellow beets

2 tablespoons olive oil

Coarse salt and freshly ground black pepper

½ pound snow peas, trimmed

½ pound jícama, peeled and cut into fine julienne

1 teaspoon grated orange zest

¾ cup fresh orange juice

2 tablespoons fresh lemon juice

¼ cup rice wine vinegar

¾ cup peanut oil

1 tablespoon sesame oil

Cayenne pepper

1 large head Boston lettuce, trimmed, leaves separated, well
washed, and dried

½ cup fresh cilantro leaves

1. Preheat the oven to 350°F.

2. Rub the beets with the olive oil and season to taste with salt and pepper. Place in a nonstick baking pan and tightly cover the pan with aluminum foil. Bake for about 35 minutes, or until just barely cooked through (the point of a small sharp knife will meet with a tiny bit of resistance in the center of the beet). Remove from the oven and allow to cool enough to handle.

3. When the beets are cool, slip off the skins and cut into fine julienne. Place in a small bowl and set aside.

4. Blanch the snow peas in rapidly boiling salted water for about 15 seconds, or until crisp-tender and bright green. Immediately drain in a fine sieve and cool under cold running water. Drain well and pat dry. Cut the snow peas into fine julienne and place in a small bowl.

5. Peel the jícama and cut it into a fine julienne. Place it in a small bowl, cover, and refrigerate until ready to use.

6. Just before serving, whisk together the orange zest, orange juice, lemon juice, vinegar, peanut oil, sesame oil, and salt and cayenne pepper to taste in a small bowl. Pour one-third over the beets, one-third over the snow peas, and the remaining one-third over the jícama.

7. Arrange the lettuce leaves on a serving platter. Place 4 evenly spaced mounds of beets on the platter at the 12, 3, 6, and 9 o'clock positions. Place a mound of half the snow peas between the 12 and 3 o'clock positions and the remaining snow peas between the 6 and 9 positions. Place a mound of half the jícama between the 3 and 6 o'clock positions and the remainder between the 9 and 12 positions. Place the cilantro in the center and serve.

Tuna and White Bean Salad

This is really an all-year-round salad. You can add seasonal vegetables, cooked potatoes, or juicy ripe tomatoes, change the tuna to swordfish or shellfish or even grilled chicken or pork, substitute black or red beans for the white, replace the parsley with cilantro or other herbs—it's up to you to make this salad your own. Instead of serving the salad on a platter, you can make individual open-faced sandwiches, or serve it on a bed of salad greens with the bread as a side. However you do it, this is one tasty salad for a weekend lunch.

SERVES 6

1 large loaf crusty Italian country bread, sliced

⅓ cup extra virgin olive oil

1½ pounds tuna steak

Coarse salt and freshly ground black pepper

3 cups cooked white beans or rinsed canned beans (about 1 cup dried)

½ cup finely chopped roasted red bell peppers (page 7)

½ cup pitted oil-cured black olives or other olives of choice

¼ cup chopped celery

4 cloves Roasted Garlic (page 6), peeled and mashed

⅓ cup white wine vinegar

2 tablespoons minced fresh flat-leaf parsley

1. Preheat the broiler. (Alternatively, preheat an outdoor grill.)

2. Using a pastry brush, generously coat both sides of the bread slices with the olive oil. Place the bread on the broiler tray and broil (or grill) for about 2 minutes per side, or until both sides are golden. Do not turn off the broiler. Line a large serving platter with the slices of toast. Set aside.

3. Using a pastry brush, lightly brush each side of the tuna steak with about 1½ teaspoons of the olive oil. Season to taste with salt and pepper.

4. Place the tuna on the broiler tray (or grill rack) and broil (or grill) for about 5 minutes, or until the first side is lightly browned. Turn and cook for an additional 3 to 5 minutes, or until an instant-read thermometer inserted into the thickest part reads 135°F for medium. (Alternatively, cook the tuna on a preheated outdoor grill or a stove-top grill or grill pan.)

5. Meanwhile, combine the beans, red peppers, olives, celery, and roasted garlic in a large bowl, tossing to combine well.

6. When the tuna is done, break it into bite-sized chunks and add it to the bean mixture.

7. Whisk together the remaining olive oil with the vinegar. Season to taste with salt and pepper and pour over the salad. Add 1 tablespoon of the parsley and toss to just combine.

8. Spoon the salad over the bread. Sprinkle the remaining 1 tablespoon parsley over the top and serve.

Tomatoes Stuffed with Shrimp Salad

Stuffed tomatoes are one of my favorite summertime specials. I can think of all measure of inventive salads to fill the centers of ripe, juicy, fresh-from-the-vine tomatoes, including salads made from grains, meat, poultry, eggs, or other vegetables. If your tomatoes are as perfect as mine, the filling will be just an accent to their sweet sun-ripened flavor.

SERVES 6

6 large very ripe tomatoes

1 avocado

1 teaspoon fresh lime juice

1 pound cooked small shrimp, peeled and deveined

1 tablespoon minced sushi (pickled) ginger

1 cup fine-quality mayonnaise

1 tablespoon minced fresh chives

Coarse salt and freshly ground black pepper

6 to 12 large lettuce leaves, washed and dried, optional

Avocado Salsa (recipe follows), optional

1. Place about four layers of paper towels on a wire rack large enough to hold the tomatoes. Cut the top quarter from each tomato. Scoop out the seeds and pulp and place the tomatoes cut side down on the rack to drain for 15 minutes. (You can, if you desire, peel the tomatoes, but peeled tomatoes are quite fragile and cannot be handled too much.)

2. Cut the avocado in half, remove the pit, and, using a spoon, scoop out the flesh onto a plate. Sprinkle the lime

juice over the top and, using a fork, mash the avocado to a very smooth consistency.

3. Place the shrimp in a medium bowl. Add the avocado and ginger and stir to blend. Stir in the mayonnaise and chives. Season to taste with salt and pepper.

4. Turn the tomatoes upright and wipe them dry. Generously fill each cavity with the shrimp salad. If desired, place each tomato on a lettuce leaf or two, garnished with the salsa, and serve. (To keep it from discoloring, sprinkle a little extra lime juice over the salsa before refrigerating.)

Avocado Salsa
MAKES ABOUT 1½ CUPS

1 cup diced avocado
1 clove garlic, minced
1 tablespoon diced red onion
1 tablespoon diced tomato
1 tablespoon fresh lime juice
1 tablespoon chopped fresh cilantro
Coarse salt and freshly ground black pepper

Combine the avocado, garlic, onion, tomato, lime juice, and cilantro in a small bowl. Season to taste with salt and pepper. Gently toss to just combine. Use immediately or cover and refrigerate for up to 8 hours.

Salmon Salad with Baby Spinach, Pea Shoots, and Artichokes

This salad takes a bit of time to put together, but it is a main course and quite filling. When you are preparing the salmon and artichokes, cook some extra for salads and sandwiches during the week. Marinate small artichokes in a tangy lemon vinaigrette and they will keep, covered and refrigerated, for a week. And, of course, any extra salmon can be made into croquettes, sandwiches, or a seafood chef's salad.

SERVES 6

Juice of 1 lemon

12 fresh tiny baby artichokes (see Note)

3 tablespoons olive oil

1 carrot, peeled and chopped

1 celery stalk, chopped

1 shallot, minced

1 cup dry white wine

1 tablespoon minced fresh flat-leaf parsley

Coarse salt and freshly ground black pepper

Six 5- to 6-ounce center-cut skinless salmon fillets, any pinbones removed

8 cups baby spinach, well washed and dried

4 cups fresh pea shoots

Black Olive Vinaigrette (recipe follows)

1. Combine the lemon juice with about 4 cups cold water in a bowl. One at a time, pull off any damaged leaves from each artichoke, trim the bottom of the stem, and peel it. To keep them from discoloring, place the artichokes in the lemon water as you work.

2. Heat 2 tablespoons of the olive oil in a medium saucepan over medium heat. Add the carrot, celery, and shallot and sauté for about 4 minutes, or just until the vegetables begin to soften.

3. Drain the artichokes and squeeze out the excess water. Add them to the saucepan and sauté for 2 minutes. Add the wine, parsley, and salt and pepper to taste and bring to a boil. Cover, lower the heat, and simmer, stirring occasionally, for about 15 minutes, or until the artichokes are tender when the stem end is pierced with a sharp knife. Remove from the heat.

4. With tongs or a slotted spoon, remove the artichokes from the cooking liquid; set the liquid aside. Carefully cut each artichoke lengthwise in half. Return the artichokes to the cooking juices to cool. When cool, drain and set aside.

5. Preheat the grill. Oil the grill rack. (Alternatively, heat a cast-iron skillet over high heat until very hot but not smoking.)

6. Rub the remaining 1 tablespoon olive oil on both sides of the salmon fillets and season to taste with salt and pepper. Place the salmon on the grill (or in the skillet) and cook for 4 minutes. Using a large spatula, carefully turn the fillets and cook for an additional 2 minutes for rare or 4 minutes for medium.

7. Meanwhile, toss the spinach and pea shoots together with about one-third of the vinaigrette. Divide the greens evenly among six plates.

8. Lay a salmon fillet in the center of each plate and drizzle the remaining vinaigrette over the top and around. Place 4 artichoke halves around the edge of each plate and serve.

NOTE: You will need artichokes that are about the size of a large walnut. If you can't find them, you can use regular artichokes, but you will have to cut the artichokes into quarters and remove the chokes (the inedible fuzzy centers). Increase the wine to 3 cups. Alternatively, you can simply purchase Italian-style artichokes packed in seasoned oil and cut them in half.

Black Olive Vinaigrette

MAKES ABOUT 1¾ CUPS

1 cup extra virgin olive oil
⅓ to ½ cup balsamic vinegar
1 tablespoon Roasted Garlic (page 6)
¼ cup black olive paste (see Note)
1 tablespoon minced capers
1 tablespoon minced sun-dried tomatoes packed in oil
Coarse salt and freshly ground black pepper

Whisk together the olive oil and vinegar in a small bowl. Whisk in the roasted garlic until well incorporated. Whisk in the olive paste, capers, and sun-dried tomatoes. Season to taste with salt and pepper.

NOTE: Black olive paste or olivada is available from specialty food stores and some supermarkets or by mail-order; see Dean & DeLuca in Sources, page 235.

Aïoli Chicken Salad

I prefer my chicken salad to be made from all parts of a freshly roasted chicken (see page 138), but I know that many eaters prefer their chicken to be white meat only. If you are one of those, be sure to poach or roast large, meaty chicken breasts on the bone for flavor. The aïoli is not a traditional French garlicky one, but it is made with sweet roasted garlic and lightened with some citrus juice. Extra salad makes a great Chicken Salad BLT (chicken salad, crisp bacon, garden-fresh lettuce, and tomatoes on toasted home-style bread).

SERVES 6

6 cups diced cooked chicken

½ cup diced celery root (or celery)

2 tablespoons minced scallions

1 tablespoon well-drained capers

1 teaspoon minced fresh tarragon

Citrus Aïoli (recipe follows)

Coarse salt and freshly ground white pepper

6 cups shredded lettuce (iceberg offers the perfect crispness)

1 tablespoon minced fresh flat-leaf parsley

1. Combine the chicken, celery root, scallions, capers, and tarragon in a large bowl. Add about 1½ cups of the aïoli and toss just to combine. (Reserve the remainder for another use.) Season to taste with salt and pepper.

2. Make a bed of the shredded lettuce on a large platter. Spoon the chicken salad into the center. Sprinkle with the parsley and serve.

Citrus Aïoli

MAKES ABOUT 2 CUPS

1 cup fresh sour orange juice (or ½ cup each fresh lemon and orange juice) (see Note)
2 large egg yolks
1½ tablespoons Roasted Garlic (page 6)
1 teaspoon Dijon mustard
Coarse salt and freshly ground black pepper
1 cup extra virgin olive oil

1. Place the orange juice in a small nonreactive saucepan over medium heat and bring to a boil. Lower the heat and simmer for about 7 minutes, or until reduced to ¼ cup. Remove from the heat and allow to cool.

2. Combine the juice, egg yolks, roasted garlic, mustard, and salt and pepper to taste in the bowl of a food processor and process until smooth. With the motor running, gradually add the oil in a slow, steady stream, processing just until the aïoli has thickened. Taste and, if necessary, adjust the seasoning with salt and pepper. Serve immediately or store, covered and refrigerated, for up to 2 days.

NOTE: Sour oranges are frequently available in Caribbean markets. They are now also grown in Florida. They have a very tangy, slightly sour orange flavor that can almost be duplicated by mixing equal portions of orange and lemon or lime juice.

If you have a concern about the safety of using uncooked eggs, use a base of about 1 cup commercial mayonnaise to which you can add the reduced juice, roasted garlic, mustard, and salt and pepper to taste.

Thai Beef and Peanut Salad

One of the thrills of living in New York City is that not only can you experience the finest "haute" cuisine in the world, but you also can find restaurants representing almost every culture in the world. In the last few years, Southeast Asian restaurants have appeared throughout the city, introducing New Yorkers to the subtle flavors of their sometimes extremely spicy cuisine. I'm not a big fan of hot food, so my version of Thai peanut salad is tamer than most, but feel free to add as much serrano chile as your heat meter can stand.

SERVES 6

1½ pounds fillet of beef (or other very tender, lean beef)

1 tablespoon olive oil

Coarse salt and freshly ground black pepper

Dressing

½ cup raspberry vinegar

½ cup tamari (see Note)

¼ cup smooth peanut butter

¼ cup black bean sauce (see Note)

1 tablespoon mirin (Japanese sweet rice wine) (see Note)

3 tablespoons minced fresh ginger, or to taste

1 teaspoon minced garlic

½ teaspoon minced serrano chile, or to taste

2 teaspoons light brown sugar

½ cup peanut oil

1 teaspoon sesame oil (see Note)

Coarse salt and freshly ground black pepper

¼ cup chopped fresh cilantro

1 pound thin spaghetti, cooked and well drained

1 cup roasted unsalted peanuts plus ½ cup chopped roasted unsalted peanuts

½ cup chopped scallions

¼ cup chopped fresh cilantro

1 bunch watercress, trimmed of tough stems, well washed, and dried, optional

1. Preheat the oven to 400°F.

2. Lightly coat the beef with the olive oil and season with salt and pepper to taste. Place in a small roasting pan and roast for about 15 minutes, or until an instant-read thermometer inserted into the center reads 140°F for rare. Remove from the oven and allow to cool to room temperature.

3. Slice the beef across the grain into very thin slices. Cut each slice into ¼-inch-wide strips. Set aside.

4. Combine the vinegar, tamari, peanut butter, black bean sauce, and mirin in a large bowl, whisking to blend well. Whisk in the ginger, garlic, and chile. Add the brown sugar, whisking until it has dissolved. Whisk in the peanut oil, sesame oil, and salt and pepper to taste. Stir in the remaining ¼ cup cilantro.

5. Add the spaghetti to the bowl, tossing to coat the strands well with the dressing. Add the beef strips, the whole peanuts, the scallions, and the cilantro and toss until well combined. Mound the salad on a serving platter and sprinkle with the chopped peanuts. If desired, garnish the platter with the watercress and serve.

NOTE: Many of these Asian ingredients are now available in most supermarkets, as well as in any Asian market and many specialty food stores. If you can't find them locally, try one of the mail-order sources on page 235.

Lunch and Brunch

I have gathered a little bit of everything from my lunch and brunch repertoire that signifies casual cooking and easy entertaining. We begin with sandwiches that start with almost-everyday burgers and tuna melts and move on to the luxury of a Lobster Club Sandwich. You are sure to find at least one sandwich that will become a house favorite. In our house, it's "Cheez Sammiches."

Then we move right along to a mélange of egg- and cheese-based dishes, tarts, pies, and stews. Most of them are easy to make and can just as readily move from the early part of the day to the dinner table. Many of these recipes are rather stick-to-your-ribs types—Cheese Strata, Scallop and Oyster Stew, and Potato-Turnip Gratin.

Although I have called for some special ingredients in a few of the recipes—such as green tomatoes (page 84) and venison (page 97)—don't hesitate to attempt the recipe if you don't have the special ingredient on hand. Go ahead and try the tart or the chili. Just use firm red tomatoes or cubed or ground beef, pork, or poultry; the results will still be fantastic.

Cheez Sammiches

A bit fancier than the grilled American cheese that seesawed with PB&J as the daily childhood fare in my boyhood home, this yummy sammich, as it's called in our house, is a favorite lunch treat. Kids of all ages love them. They're hearty enough to make a full meal when accompanied by a bowl of soup or a green salad. I use any kind of soft cheese (except American. Well, the boys do ask for American cheese so what can I do?), sometimes even a pricey French triple crème. Whatever smoked meat I have on hand and any richly flavored mustard will change the flavor, but not the savor, of this filling sandwich. A big bowl of crunchy pickles is put on the table when we eat ours. You can call it a sandwich, but if you sit at our table, you will have to call it a sammich.

SERVES 6

3 cups grated or chopped cheese (such as Gruyère, Cantal, Manchego, Brie, farmhouse cheddar)

1 cup minced cooked ham or other cooked or smoked meat

3 tablespoons milk

2 tablespoons grated onion

2 tablespoons prepared mustard, plus extra for serving

½ teaspoon well-drained bottled horseradish, optional (for adults)

12 slices whole-grain or sourdough raisin bread

3 tablespoons unsalted butter, softened

1. Combine the cheese, meat, milk, onion, mustard, and optional horseradish in a medium bowl. Stir until very well blended. Generously spread the mixture on 6 slices of the bread. Top with the remaining bread. Generously butter both sides of each sandwich.

2. Preheat a griddle over medium heat. When hot, add as many sandwiches will fit on the griddle without crowding. Toast for about 3 minutes per side, or until the bread is golden and crisp and the cheese has melted. Remove the sandwiches from the griddle and keep warm in a low oven while you toast the remaining sandwiches.

3. Slice each sandwich on the diagonal and serve, with additional mustard and, if desired, crunchy pickles.

Tomato–Goat Cheese Melts

Only in the summer. I say that over and over when it comes to tomatoes. No matter how often we hear about a new hybrid "keeper" from growers and botanists, they don't seem to be able to create the deep, sweet flavor of a just-picked, late-July tomato. This sandwich came about when I had picked some particularly ripe tomatoes and a friend had given me some freshly made farmstead goat cheese. I've served it for breakfast, brunch, lunch, and even for a light supper, with a salad and some ice-cold beer.

SERVES 6

6 English muffins

About 2 to 3 very ripe large beefsteak tomatoes

Approximately ½ cup Dijon or other strong-flavored mustard

2 cups arugula leaves, well washed and dried

Coarse salt and freshly ground black pepper

3 tablespoons extra virgin olive oil

1 pound fresh goat cheese

½ cup dry bread crumbs

1. Preheat the oven to 375°F.

2. Split the English muffins in half and lightly toast them.

3. Peel and core the tomatoes. Cut them crosswise into ½- to ¾-inch-thick slices and remove the seeds.

4. Generously coat the cut sides of the toasted muffins with mustard. Place a few arugula leaves on top of each and then

place a tomato slice on top. Lightly season with salt and pepper. Using a pastry brush, lightly coat the tomatoes with the olive oil.

5. Place the muffins on a baking sheet and bake for about 12 minutes, or until the tomatoes are beginning to soften. Remove from the oven and generously crumble the goat cheese over the tomatoes. Sprinkle the bread crumbs over the top and bake for an additional 5 minutes, or until the cheese has melted and the tops are golden. Serve immediately.

Great Burgers on the Grill

What would life be without big, fat, juicy burgers hot off the grill? At our house, burgers are one of the first meals to be grilled once the snow melts. I combine ground sirloin and chuck for these so the burgers have the rich, meaty flavor of the sirloin and the fat of the chuck for juiciness. You can make classic burgers for the kids and, with my variations, go hog-wild for the adults. If you put enough garnishes on the table, you don't really have to make anything else, but I do love a side of Potato Salad (page 42).

SERVES 6

1 pound lean ground beef sirloin

1 pound ground beef chuck

Coarse salt and freshly ground black pepper

6 hamburger rolls, split and toasted

Garnishes (see Note)

1. Preheat a grill. Oil the grill rack.

2. Combine the sirloin, chuck, 2 tablespoons ice water, and salt and pepper to taste in a medium bowl. Form the meat into 6 patties.

3. Place the patties on the hot grill and grill, turning once, for about 4 minutes per side for rare or 5 minutes per side for medium. Place each burger on a toasted bun and serve with the inevitable bottle of Heinz and whatever garnishes you choose.

NOTE: For garnishes, choose sliced tomatoes, lettuce leaves, sliced sweet or red onion (raw or grilled), pickles, relish, sautéed mushrooms, chili, bacon, mustard, mayonnaise, and/or salsa.

For variations on the burger theme, add to the meat: ½ cup minced red onion and/or 2 tablespoons minced fresh herbs, such as parsley, chives, rosemary, and/or thyme

OR ½ cup minced onion, 2 tablespoons minced fresh cilantro and minced garlic and jalapeño or other chile pepper to taste

OR ½ cup ketchup, 2 tablespoons dark beer, 1 tablespoon Worcestershire sauce, 1 tablespoon Dijon mustard, 1 tablespoon minced onion, and ¾ cup dried bread crumbs.

OR form each patty around a 1-inch square of cheese (cheddar, Jack, Brie, blue, goat, etc.), or, about a minute before the burgers are ready to come off the grill, place a thick slice of any type of cheese you like on top of each and allow it to melt.

Other meats such as lamb and pork make great burgers, as do chicken and turkey. However, pork, chicken, and turkey have so little fat that I usually sauté some minced onion in 3 to 4 tablespoons of oil and add it to the meat before I make the patties so the grilled burgers have a bit of juiciness.

Portobello mushrooms also make great burgers. Choose large, fat mushrooms, remove the stems, and wipe the caps clean. Marinate in a combination of balsamic vinegar, olive oil, minced fresh thyme and flat-leaf parsley, and salt and pepper to taste for about 15 minutes before grilling. Garnish the burgers with arugula or other spicy greens and roasted red peppers.

Lobster Club Sandwich

Very simple, and, yes, very expensive. It doesn't take a lot of effort, but it does require the absolute best of ingredients. This sandwich was, as far as I know, introduced by Anne Rosenzweig, a marvelous New York chef, at her restaurant Arcadia. It was so popular that she eventually opened another restaurant called Lobster Club. Since its introduction, the lobster club sandwich has appeared on many, many menus and most chefs wonder why they didn't think of it first. It is my favorite luxury sandwich!

SERVES 6

1½ pounds cooked lobster meat, cut into small cubes

1 cup Citrus Aïoli (page 64) or any rich mayonnaise (see Note)

Coarse salt and freshly ground white pepper

18 thin slices home-style white bread, toasted

1 head butter lettuce, trimmed, pulled apart, well washed, and dried

3 to 4 very ripe yellow or orange heirloom tomatoes, sliced about ¼ inch thick (see Note)

18 slices thick-sliced bacon, crisply cooked and drained (see Note)

1. In a medium bowl, gently toss the lobster with ¾ cup of the aïoli. Season to taste with salt and pepper. Lay 6 slices of the toast out on a work surface. Generously mound the lobster onto the slices of toast. Top with a leaf or two of lettuce. Lightly spread some of the remaining aïoli on 6 of the remaining pieces of toast. Place aïoli side down on top of the lettuce and lightly spread the top of each with aïoli. Layer 1 or 2 slices of tomato (depending upon the size of the slices),

3 strips of bacon, and a couple of lettuce leaves on top. Spread the remaining aïoli on the remaining 6 slices of toast. Place the toast aïoli side down on top of the sandwiches.

2. Holding the sandwich together, carefully cut each one into triangles (or anchor with toothpicks, then slice). Place a toothpick in each triangle to secure it. Serve immediately.

NOTE: If you don't have time to make the aïoli, try one of the delicious commercially prepared mayonnaises flavored with lemon, garlic, or herbs.

I have chosen yellow or orange tomatoes for their color and for the fact that they usually aren't quite as juicy as red tomatoes, but feel free to substitute beefsteak tomatoes.

You can use crisply fried thin slices of pancetta, Canadian bacon, or country ham in place of the bacon.

Mile-High Shrimp Sandwiches

These are great Saturday night sandwiches. Why Saturday night? Just 'cause it's a great night to watch some classic movies and have a sandwich supper. (Since I am usually working in one of my restaurants on Saturday night, my Saturday night is usually Sunday.) Whatever day you choose to make them, you will find these shrimp sandwiches are the premier open-faced meal. You can prepare the shrimp in any way you like, but hot off the grill is best. The blue cheese dressing makes a great sandwich spread.

SERVES 6

1 large carrot, peeled and julienned

1/4 cup julienned red onion

2 teaspoons fresh lemon juice

2 teaspoons light brown sugar

1/2 teaspoon grated fresh ginger

Pinch of cayenne pepper, or to taste

Coarse salt

1 avocado

Juice of 1 lime

6 large slices sourdough or other coarse, crusty bread, lightly toasted

1 package radish or alfalfa sprouts

1½ pounds cooked medium shrimp, peeled and deveined

Blue Cheese Dressing (recipe follows)

1. Blanch the carrots in rapidly boiling salted water for about 30 seconds, or until the color is set but the carrots are still very crisp. Drain well and cool under cold running water. Pat dry.

2. Combine the carrots, onion, lemon juice, brown sugar, ginger, and cayenne in a small bowl and toss to mix. Season with salt and additional cayenne if necessary. Set aside. (The salad can be made early in the day, covered, and refrigerated.)

3. Halve the avocado, remove the pit, and scoop the flesh into a small bowl. Mash the avocado, then add the lime juice and salt to taste and stir to combine.

4. Lay the toast out on a work surface. Spread the mashed avocado on top of the slices. Lightly mound some sprouts on the avocado. Sprinkle with the carrot salad. Arrange the shrimp over the salad and generously drizzle the dressing over the top. Serve immediately.

Blue Cheese Dressing

MAKES ABOUT 2 CUPS

¾ cup creamed cottage cheese
¼ cup sour cream
2 tablespoons buttermilk
Tabasco sauce
1 cup crumbled Maytag Blue cheese or other fine-quality blue cheese

Place the cottage cheese, sour cream, buttermilk, and Tabasco to taste in the bowl of a food processor and process until very smooth. Scrape the mixture into a small bowl. Fold in the blue cheese. Allow to stand at room temperature for 30 minutes before using as a salad dressing or a sandwich spread. (The dressing can be made up to 3 days in advance and stored tightly covered and refrigerated.)

Crispy Oysters and Citrus Mayonnaise on a Bulkie

What's a bulkie, you say? A bulkie is just another name for a roll—usually a seeded round roll, but it can also be what, in New York City, we call a hero or a sub—a small loaf of Italian bread. In this recipe, I opt for the seeded round roll. You don't need to shuck the oysters yourself; you can buy preshucked ones from most reputable fish markets or even from some supermarket fish departments. The oysters, without the roll, make great pop-in-your-mouth accompaniments for sparkling wine.

SERVES 6

2 cups buttermilk

2½ cups Wondra flour

1 teaspoon grated lemon zest

1 teaspoon minced fresh tarragon

Coarse salt and freshly ground black pepper

Approximately 6 cups vegetable oil

3 dozen large oysters, shucked, well drained, and patted dry

6 seeded round rolls, split, toasted if desired

Citrus Mayonnaise (recipe follows)

1. Preheat the oven to low or warm.

2. Place the buttermilk in a medium bowl. Combine the flour, lemon zest, tarragon, and salt and pepper to taste in a sealable plastic bag.

3. Heat the oil in a deep heavy saucepan or deep-fat fryer over high heat until a thermometer reads 365°F.

4. While the oil is heating, coat the oysters. Dip a few at a time into the buttermilk, then toss them in the seasoned flour (seal the bag as you toss to keep the flour from flying around). Remove from the flour and shake off any excess. Set the coated oysters on a baking sheet as you go.

5. Place the oysters, a few at a time, in the hot oil and fry, turning as necessary, for about 2 minutes, or until just cooked and golden brown. Using a slotted spoon, remove the oysters from the oil and drain on paper towels. Then place on a baking sheet and keep warm in the preheated oven while you fry the remaining oysters.

6. Pile some oysters on the bottom half of each roll—don't be skimpy! Spoon some mayonnaise over the oysters and cover with the tops of the rolls, gently pushing the halves together. Cut in half and serve.

Citrus Mayonnaise
MAKES ABOUT 2 CUPS

1 medium orange
¾ cup fine-quality mayonnaise
1 teaspoon fresh lemon juice
¼ teaspoon sesame oil, or to taste
1 teaspoon minced shallot
Tabasco sauce
1 teaspoon minced fresh dill

1. Grate 1 teaspoon zest from the orange; set aside. Using a sharp knife, cut the peel and white pith from the orange. Slice between the membranes to release the orange segments and chop them into very small pieces, discarding any seeds. Place the flesh in a fine sieve set over a bowl and allow the juice to drain off for about 15 minutes.

2. Combine the mayonnaise, lemon juice, and sesame oil in a small bowl and blend well. Beat in the reserved orange zest, the shallots, and Tabasco to taste. Fold in the drained orange flesh and the dill. Use immediately or cover and refrigerate for up to 2 days.

Tuna Melts—My Way

I confess to a weakness for diner-style tuna melts made with tuna salad and American cheese. My tuna melts, however, elevate this American classic to new levels. I spread some tapenade on warm sourdough toast, and layer on thick fresh tuna steaks with a melt of Fontina cheese. Add an ice-cold beer and turn on the game.

SERVES 6

1 cup chopped pitted oil-cured black olives

½ cup chopped roasted red bell peppers packed in oil, well drained (page 7)

2 tablespoons well-drained capers

1 tablespoon Roasted Garlic (page 6)

4 anchovies packed in oil, well drained and patted dry

2 tablespoons olive oil

1 teaspoon fresh lemon juice

Coarse salt and freshly ground black pepper

Six 4-ounce tuna steaks, about 1½ inches thick

1 tablespoon vegetable oil

6 slices sourdough toast

12 slices Fontina cheese

1. Place the olives, roasted peppers, capers, roasted garlic, anchovies, olive oil, and lemon juice in the bowl of a food processor and pulse to a coarse paste. Season to taste with salt and pepper. Set aside.

2. Preheat the broiler.

3. Season the tuna steaks with salt and pepper to taste. Heat the vegetable oil in a large sauté pan over medium-high heat. Add the tuna, without crowding, and sear for 3 minutes, or until a slight crust forms on the bottom. Turn and sear the other side for 3 minutes for rare or 5 minutes for medium. Remove from the pan and let rest for a couple of minutes.

4. Liberally mound some of the olive mixture on each piece of toast. Lay a tuna steak on top and place 2 slices of Fontina cheese on top of the tuna. Place the sandwiches under the broiler for about 2 minutes, or until the cheese begins to bubble and color. Remove from the broiler and serve immediately.

Frittata

Frittatas, big, open-faced omelets, are perfect crowd food. All you need is a dozen farm-fresh eggs and some cheese, vegetables, or meat. Even leftover vegetables and meats are a welcome addition. Frittatas are easier to cook than the traditional folded French omelet. There is no filling and flipping. They can be eaten hot, warm, or at room temperature. You can serve frittatas at any time of the day, from breakfast to a Saturday night after-the-movies supper. The one thing you do need is a large nonstick ovenproof skillet.

SERVES 6 TO 8

5 tablespoons olive oil

1 cup coarsely chopped onions or leeks

¼ cup diced red bell pepper, optional

1 teaspoon minced garlic

1½ pounds thinly sliced summer squash, potatoes, asparagus, chopped artichoke hearts, broccoli, and/or cauliflower

Coarse salt and freshly ground black pepper

12 large eggs

½ cup half-and-half

¼ cup freshly grated Parmesan cheese

1 tablespoon chopped fresh basil

1 tablespoon chopped fresh flat-leaf parsley

1. Heat 2 tablespoons of the olive oil in a large sauté pan over medium heat. Add the onions and, if using, the bell pepper and sauté for 5 minutes. Add the garlic and sauté for another minute. Stir in the vegetables and season to taste with salt

and pepper. Cover and cook for 5 minutes, or until the vegetables are just cooked through. Time will depend on the vegetable—summer squash will take no more than 5 minutes, potatoes may take 20—so start cooking with the firmer vegetables first. Remove from the heat, pour the mixture into a fine sieve set over a bowl, and allow it to drain for 15 minutes.

2. Preheat the oven to 400°F.

3. Beat together the eggs, half-and-half, Parmesan cheese, basil, and parsley in a large bowl. Stir in the vegetable mixture and adjust the seasoning with salt and pepper.

4. Heat the remaining 3 tablespoons olive oil in a large nonstick ovenproof skillet over medium heat. Pour in the egg mixture, lower the heat, and cook for about 10 minutes, or until the bottom is set and beginning to brown and the top is just beginning to set.

5. Place the pan in the oven and bake for about 10 minutes, or until the center of the frittata is just set. (If the top is not brown, raise the oven temperature to broil and place the frittata under the broiler for a minute or two.) Remove from the oven and allow to rest for 5 minutes. Cut into wedges and serve.

Green Tomato Tart

When tomatoes are just beginning to ripen on the vine, I can't resist picking a few big, fat green ones to fry or to use in a tart. My rationale is that there are always too many tomatoes to eat once the ripening begins so I am doing just a little natural culling. If the only way you have enjoyed green tomatoes is fried, then this savory tart is the perfect introduction. It is a brunch-lunch standout.

MAKES ONE 10-INCH TART, 6 TO 8 SERVINGS

½ recipe Flaky Pie Pastry (page 205)

1 large egg yolk, beaten with 1 teaspoon water for egg wash

3 medium green tomatoes

4 thick slices bacon, cut crosswise into 1-inch pieces

3 large eggs

1½ cups half-and-half or heavy cream

Coarse salt and freshly ground black pepper

1 cup grated Gruyère or sharp cheddar cheese or crumbled goat cheese

1. Preheat the oven to 350°F.

2. Roll out the pastry on a lightly floured board to a circle about 12 inches in diameter. Carefully lift the pastry circle and fit it into a 10-inch tart pan (with a removable bottom); fold and press any excess dough into the fluted edge. Using a pastry brush, coat the bottom of the pastry shell with the egg wash. Set aside.

3. Core and cut the tomatoes crosswise into thin slices. Place the slices on a double layer of paper towels to drain.

4. Fry the bacon in a large sauté pan over medium heat, stirring frequently, for about 8 minutes, or until it is crisp and has rendered all of its fat. Using a slotted spoon, lift the bacon from the pan and place it on paper towels to drain.

5. Using a whisk, beat the eggs with the half-and-half in a medium bowl until very well blended. Season to taste with salt and pepper, keeping in mind that you will be adding bacon and cheese to the mixture, which will add more salt.

6. Spread the cheese over the bottom of the prepared pastry shell. Using paper towels, pat the tomatoes as dry as possible, then carefully lay them, in slightly overlapping concentric circles, on the cheese. Pour the egg mixture over the tomatoes. Crumble the bacon over the top.

7. Bake for about 35 minutes, or until the custard has set and is lightly browned on top. Remove from the oven and allow to rest for 5 minutes. Cut into wedges and serve with a green salad, warm rolls, and wine or cold beer.

Pissaladière

Rather than Italian-style pizza, in our house we make pissaladière, a French-style pizza tart that I learned to make while cooking in France. It is traditionally made with anchovies, but since they are an "iffy" item with the kids, I use sun-dried tomatoes—which are more than equal to the briny saltiness of cured anchovies. If you love anchovies, use them, or add some dried sausage or crumbled fresh Italian sausage for a heartier pie. Any roasted vegetable would also make a great topping. Since pissaladière can be eaten either warm or at room temperature, it is ideal on a busy weekend.

SERVES 6

3 pounds sweet onions such as Vidalia or Maui

3 tablespoons extra virgin olive oil

3 cloves garlic, minced

1 tablespoon herbes de Provence (see Note)

¼ teaspoon ground cloves

Coarse salt and freshly ground black pepper

Approximately ¼ cup yellow cornmeal

½ recipe Pizza Dough (recipe follows)

1 cup pitted Niçoise olives

½ cup well-drained sun-dried tomatoes packed in oil, cut into thin strips

1. Preheat the oven to 375°F.

2. Slice the onions paper-thin. Pull the rings apart and place them in a large shallow dish. Add the olive oil, garlic,

herbes de Provence, and cloves and toss well. Season to taste with salt and pepper.

3. Spread the onions out on a baking sheet. Bake, stirring frequently, for about 25 minutes, or until the onions are quite soft and slightly caramelized and the moisture has almost completely evaporated. Remove the onions from the oven. Raise the oven temperature to 475°F.

4. Sprinkle an 11 × 17-inch baking sheet or jelly-roll pan with cornmeal. Place the dough in the pan and pat it evenly over the bottom and up the sides of the pan. Crimp the edges against the top of the pan.

5. Spread the cooked onion mixture over the dough. Sprinkle the olives and sun-dried tomatoes over the top.

6. Bake for about 20 minutes, or until the crust is cooked through and the edges are golden brown. Remove from the oven and cut into square or triangular pieces. Serve warm or at room temperature.

NOTE: Herbes de Provence is a classic herb mixture in southern France. It is available in the spice section of many supermarkets and in specialty food stores.

Pizza Dough

MAKES ENOUGH FOR 2 LARGE PIZZAS

3 cups all-purpose flour
Approximately ¾ cup semolina flour
2 tablespoons rapid-rise yeast
1 teaspoon fine sea salt
1 tablespoon honey
1 tablespoon extra virgin olive oil

1. Combine the flours, yeast, and salt in a large bowl. Stir the honey, olive oil, and 1½ cups warm water together until well combined. With a large wooden spoon, beat the liquid into the flour.

2. Scoop the dough out onto a lightly floured board and, using your hands, knead the dough until it is smooth and elastic. If the dough seems too wet, add up to an additional ¼ cup semolina flour, no more. (Alternatively, if you have a large heavy-duty electric mixer, you can make the dough in it.)

3. Divide the dough in half and form it into 2 large, flat rounds. Place each one on a lightly floured baking sheet. Cover and allow to rise in a warm, draft-free spot until doubled in volume, about 2 hours.

4. Working with one circle of dough at a time, lightly flour your hands and lift the dough from the baking sheet by placing your fists underneath it. Begin stretching the dough by simultaneously turning the circle and pulling your fists away from the center. Reflour your hands if necessary as you pull the dough out to fit the pan, with the dough no more than ¼ inch thick. (You will only need one circle of dough to make the crust for the pissaladière. The remaining dough can be kept, tightly covered and refrigerated, for up to 2 days, or it can be frozen.)

5. If the above method seems too difficult, sprinkle equal portions of flour and cornmeal (about ½ cup total) onto a cool work surface. Turn the dough circle out onto the floured surface and turn to coat. Gently flatten the dough circle some-what with the palms of your hands. Then use a rolling pin to flatten the dough to the appropriate size. When doing this, roll lightly, as you don't want to com-press the dough, or it will toughen. Transfer the dough to the pan and, if neces-sary, crimp the edges into the pan.

NOTE: The pizza dough can be used to make two regular tomato-mozzarella pizzas.

Potato-Turnip Gratin

I came to love gratins during my early learning-to-cook visits to France. It took me a while to figure out that my Mom's scalloped potatoes had their origin in these classic French dishes and that I had in fact been eating them all my life. You can make a gratin out of almost anything—potatoes, leeks, turnips, spinach.

At home, we often have a gratin for a cold, gray-day late Sunday lunch with a salad of bitter winter greens and some warm, crusty bread. Gratins can be put together in the morning, then popped in the oven later in the day. They are rich, creamy, and filling and I haven't met anyone who doesn't love them.

SERVES 6

1 cup heavy cream

4 large cloves Roasted Garlic (page 6), peeled

1½ pounds Idaho potatoes

1 pound white turnips, peeled, cut crosswise into ⅛-inch-thick slices, and patted dry

4 tablespoons (½ stick) unsalted butter, softened

1 cup grated Emmenthaler cheese (see Note)

Ground nutmeg

Coarse salt and freshly ground black pepper

¼ cup fresh bread crumbs

1. Preheat the oven to 425°F. Lightly butter a 10 x 2-inch oval gratin dish. Set aside.

2. Heat the cream in a small saucepan until hot. Remove from the heat and whisk in the roasted garlic until well blended. Set aside.

3. Peel the potatoes and cut them crosswise into ⅛-inch-thick slices. Using a clean kitchen towel, pat the slices very dry. Place the potatoes in a large bowl, add the turnips, and toss to combine.

4. Place a layer of the potato-turnip mixture in the bottom of the prepared dish. Dot the top with half of the butter, sprinkle with half the cheese, and season with nutmeg and salt and pepper to taste. Arrange the remaining potato-turnip mixture over the first layer, top with the remaining butter and cheese, and season with nutmeg and salt and pepper to taste. Pour the garlic-flavored cream over the top and sprinkle the bread crumbs evenly over the top.

5. Bake the gratin for 45 minutes, or until the vegetables are tender, the cream has been absorbed, and the top is bubbling and golden brown. Remove from the oven and let the gratin rest for 5 minutes before serving directly from the dish.

NOTE: You can use any type of cheese that has a bit of a bite to it. Goat cheeses, soft or hard, add a wonderfully intriguing flavor.

Cheese Strata

My mom's version of cheese strata, simply referred to as "Mom's Cheese Dish," is really nothing more than a savory bread pudding and a great way to use leftover bread. Mom could be counted on to bring this favorite to large family gatherings or drop it off to a neighbor in need. I like her version, but with the addition of brown sugar, mustard, and two kinds of cheese, mine has more depth of flavor. Perfect for a winter's brunch, lunch, or a light supper or great to make on the weekend for serving during the busy week ahead, it can be put together and then covered and refrigerated for a day or two before baking. Use an overproof casserole that can go from the cold refrigerator to the hot oven.

SERVES 6 TO 8

3 tablespoons unsalted butter

12 slices stale bread, crusts trimmed off and cut into small cubes

8 large eggs

1 tablespoon grated onion

3½ cups half-and-half

1 teaspoon light brown sugar

1 teaspoon dry mustard

1 teaspoon Worcestershire sauce

¼ teaspoon paprika

Dash of Tabasco sauce

Coarse salt and freshly ground black pepper

¾ pound sharp cheddar cheese, grated

¾ pound Monterey Jack cheese, grated

1. Melt 2 tablespoons of the butter in a large sauté pan over medium heat. Add the bread cubes and sauté for about 3 minutes, or until the bread has absorbed the butter. Remove from the heat.

2. Whisk together the eggs, onion, half-and-half, sugar, mustard, Worcestershire sauce, paprika, Tabasco, and salt and pepper to taste in a large bowl until well combined. Combine the cheddar and Jack cheeses, tossing to mix.

3. Preheat the oven to 350°F.

4. Using the remaining 1 tablespoon butter, generously butter a 3-quart deep casserole.

5. Place one-third of the bread cubes in the bottom of the prepared casserole. Sprinkle with half of the cheese. Place another third of the cubes on top of the cheese, spreading them out to cover. Top with a layer of the remaining cheese and then with a final layer of bread cubes. Pour the egg mixture over the top. Cover and let stand for 15 minutes.

6. Bake the casserole for 45 minutes, or until the top is bubbly and golden brown. Remove from the heat and allow to rest for 10 minutes. Serve hot.

NOTE: Minced ham, cooked crumbled bacon, chopped roasted bell or chile peppers, chopped scallions, or chopped broccoli can be added to the cheese layers.

Winter-Vegetable Shepherd's Pie

Rather than the ubiquitous English-style dish with ground lamb or beef, I make my shepherd's pie with winter vegetables braised in chicken broth and herbs (use vegetable broth for a vegetarian version). Topped with soothing mashed potatoes, this is a weekend favorite. Since we are a meat-and-potatoes kind of family, I often serve it as an accompaniment to Perfect Roast Chicken (page 138). With a salad of bitter winter greens, this can be a main course too.

SERVES 6

2 cups diced parsnips

2 cups diced carrots

1 cup diced yellow beets

1 cup diced rutabaga

12 pearl onions, peeled

6 cloves Roasted Garlic (page 6), peeled

3 cups chopped Swiss chard stems and leaves

1 teaspoon minced fresh tarragon

1 teaspoon minced fresh flat-leaf parsley

Coarse salt and freshly ground black pepper

6 tablespoons unsalted butter, melted

3 cups chicken broth

4 cups mashed potatoes (page 105)

¼ cup fresh bread crumbs

1. Preheat the oven to 350°F. Lightly grease a 3-quart deep casserole. Set aside.

2. Toss the parsnips, carrots, beets, rutabaga, pearl onions, and garlic together in a large bowl. Add the chard, tarragon, parsley, salt and pepper to taste, and ¼ cup of the melted butter. Transfer the mixture to the prepared casserole and add the chicken broth. Cover the casserole tightly with aluminum foil.

3. Bake for about 35 minutes, or until all of the vegetables are tender. Remove the casserole from the oven and remove the foil. Do not turn the oven off.

4. Cover the vegetables with the mashed potatoes. Brush the top with the remaining 2 tablespoons melted butter and sprinkle with the bread crumbs. Return to the oven for about 15 minutes, or until the potatoes are golden brown and crusty. Serve hot.

Scallop and Oyster Stew

Scallops are one of my very favorite seafoods, so much so that the signature dish at my restaurant Aureole is a sea scallop sandwich. One weekend I felt a hunger for oyster stew, but none of the seafood stores had enough oysters to answer my urge, so I substituted some small East Coast scallops known as bay scallops. They are quite a bit sweeter and juicier than the more common and larger sea scallops. If only sea scallops are available, cut them into half-inch pieces before cooking them. This rich, hearty stew makes a great supper or brunch dish.

SERVES 6

¼ pound pancetta, finely diced

1 tablespoon unsalted butter

¼ cup finely diced shallots

¼ cup finely diced carrots

¼ cup finely diced fennel

½ teaspoon minced fresh tarragon

½ cup Riesling

2 cups half-and-half

2 cups heavy cream

24 oysters, shucked and juices reserved

1 pound bay scallops

Coarse salt and freshly ground white pepper

1 tablespoon minced fennel fronds

1. Place the pancetta in a medium sauté pan over medium heat and sauté for about 10 minutes, or until the pancetta is crisp and all of its fat has rendered. Using a slotted spoon, lift the pancetta from the pan and place it on a double layer of paper towels to drain.

2. Melt the butter in a large saucepan over medium heat. Add the shallots, carrots, fennel, and tarragon and sauté for about 6 minutes, or until the vegetables are quite soft. Add the wine and cook for another 5 minutes, or until most of the wine has evaporated. Add the half-and-half and cream and bring to just a bare simmer; do not boil. Gently simmer for 3 minutes.

3. Add the oysters, along with their juices, and the scallops, season to taste with salt and pepper, and simmer for about 1 minute, or just until the shellfish is cooked. Stir in the fennel fronds and the pancetta and serve immediately.

NOTE: For a lighter stew, replace half of the half-and-half and cream with 2 cups fish stock or clam juice.

If you prefer a thicker stew, make a mixture of 1 tablespoon of all-purpose flour worked into 1 tablespoon softened unsalted butter and whisk it into the stew before you add the shellfish.

Venison Chili

Every fall, my brothers and I went hunting with our dad, and in good years, we ate venison all winter in stews, soups, and burgers. Nowadays farmed venison is available all year long from butchers and specialty food stores. Venison chili has remained a family favorite. As I learned more about seasonings, I fooled with my mom's basic recipe, but the idea remains true—a huge pot of hearty, crowd-pleasing, warmly spiced chili. The optional jalapeño adds some heat to this gently seasoned brew. A pan of freshly baked corn bread and a salad of romaine make a complete meal.

SERVES 6 TO 8

½ pound (about 1 cup) dried black beans, rinsed and picked clean

2 tablespoons canola oil, or more as needed

2 pounds boneless venison steak, cut into small cubes

Coarse salt and freshly ground black pepper

1 large onion, chopped

1 red bell pepper, cored, seeded, and chopped

1 tablespoon minced garlic

1 jalapeño chile, or to taste, seeded and minced, optional

2 tablespoons ground chile powder (see Note)

2 teaspoons ground cumin

1 teaspoon dried oregano

One 28-ounce can tomatoes, chopped, with their juice

½ cup chipotle chiles in adobo (see Note)

1 tablespoon tomato paste

One 12-ounce bottle dark beer

1 cup shredded cheddar or Monterey Jack cheese or crumbled goat cheese, optional

1 cup sour cream or homemade crème fraîche (see page 8) or store-bought crème
       fraîche, optional

1. Place the beans in a large saucepan with cold water to cover by 3 inches and allow them to soak for at least 8 hours or overnight.

2. Leaving the beans in their soaking water, place the saucepan over high heat and bring to a boil. Lower the heat and simmer for about 45 minutes, or until the beans are tender. Remove from the heat and set aside.

3. Heat the oil in a Dutch oven over medium heat. Pat the venison dry and season it to taste with salt and pepper. Place the meat in the pot without crowding (in batches, if necessary) and sauté for about 5 minutes, or until nicely browned; you may have to use additional oil to keep the meat from sticking. Remove the meat from the pot as it is browned.

4. When all of the meat has been browned, add the onion, bell pepper, garlic, and optional jalapeño to the Dutch oven and sauté for 5 minutes. Return the meat to the pot and add the chile powder, cumin, and oregano, stirring to combine well. Add the tomatoes, chipotle chiles, and tomato paste and stir to blend. Add the beer and the beans, with their cooking liquid, and bring to a boil. Lower the heat and simmer for about 2 hours, or until the chili is very thick and the meat is almost falling apart (see Note).

5. Serve hot, topped with cheese and a dollop of sour cream or crème fraîche, if desired.

NOTE: Be sure to use a pure chile powder, such as that ground from New Mexico, pasilla, árbol, or California chiles, available from Latin markets, specialty food stores, and some supermarkets. If you can't find pure ground dried chiles, use the commercially blended chili powder, but do not add the cumin until after the chili has cooked a bit. Because most commercial blends include cumin, you will need to give a taste and decide whether you should add some or all of the cumin called for in the recipe.

Chipotle chiles in adobo are chiles canned in a seasoned tomato sauce. They are available from Latin markets, specialty food stores, and many supermarkets.

All chilies are best made a day or two in advance and reheated just before serving. This gives the flavors a chance to meld together for a more subtle taste.

Speidies

In central New York State, where I grew up, summertime is speidie-time. Speidies are beef or chicken kabobs marinated in a locally produced speidie sauce. Nobody makes their own; everybody buys it by the case to make it through the summer's grilling. Now that I live downstate, I've had to devise my own speidie sauce (really nothing more than a quite acidic vinaigrette), which I'm willing to share for the very first time.

MAKES 12

2 cups dry white wine

1/4 cup sherry wine vinegar

1/4 cup vegetable oil

1/2 cup minced shallots

1 tablespoon minced garlic

1 tablespoon minced fresh flat-leaf parsley

2 bay leaves, crumbled

1/4 teaspoon dried thyme

1/4 teaspoon dried oregano

Coarse salt and freshly ground white pepper

1 1/2 to 2 pounds boneless, skinless chicken or turkey or very lean boneless beef, lamb, or pork, cut into 1 1/2- to 2-inch cubes

24 cherry tomatoes, optional

24 small button mushrooms, trimmed and brushed clean, optional

Twenty-four 1-inch squares red or yellow bell pepper, optional

12 pita breads, toasted, optional

1. Combine the wine, vinegar, and oil in a medium bowl or other nonreactive container. Stir in the shallots, garlic, parsley, bay leaves, thyme, oregano, and salt and white pepper to taste. Cover and allow the flavors to blend for at least 1 hour before using. (The marinade can be covered and refrigerated for up to 1 week.)

2. If you are using wooden skewers, place them in cold water to cover for at least 1 hour. Remove the skewers from the water just before you are ready to use them.

3. One to two hours before you are ready to grill, place the poultry or meat in a shallow nonreactive container. Pour the speidie sauce over the top. Cover with plastic wrap and refrigerate for up to 2 hours, turning occasionally. If using the vegetables, add them to the marinade with the meat about 15 minutes before you are ready to grill.

4. Preheat the grill. Oil the grill rack.

5. Thread the poultry or meat cubes (and vegetables, if using) onto skewers, (alternating poultry or meat with the vegetables, if using, and beginning and ending with poultry or meat). If using wooden skewers, you might want to wrap the tips in aluminum foil to keep them from burning. Place the kabobs on the grill and grill, turning frequently, for about 8 minutes, or until the meat is cooked to the desired degree of doneness (and the vegetables are crisp-tender). Serve hot off the grill, with toasted pita bread, if desired.

Vegetables and Sides

If you have children, you know how hard it can be to get them to eat their vegetables. Using many of the recipes in this chapter, we've been pretty successful in getting our kids—as well as adults—to ask for seconds. A little balsamic vinegar, a touch of garlic, a mellow vinaigrette, or a hint of citrus are just a few of the Palmer tricks to make vegetables show their true and very tasty colors.

I have also included a couple of not-so-expected side dishes—stuffing for poultry and macaroni and cheese. I thought about putting the macaroni with the pastas, and then I considered lunch and brunch dishes, but in my mom's house, macaroni and cheese was always a side dish. We were such a meat-and-potatoes family that mom never dared set a table without meat in the center. So, a side dish it remains. My Super Macaroni and Cheese is a few steps up from my mom's, so you might even want to feature it at the center of the table. I'm sure it will satisfy the most ravenous eater. And I should know, since it is often my late-night after-work snack.

Talking Potatoes

Potatoes, just about my most favorite part of a meal, are particularly well suited to casual cooking since leftover potatoes can be turned into hash browns, added to frittatas, or used as a shepherd's pie topping. I usually allow 1 medium to large potato per person with a couple of extra ones thrown in for seconds. Sometimes I double the number of potatoes to ensure that I'll have leftovers to expand my repertoire.

Any potato, except the mealier Idaho or baking potatoes, can be placed in a steamer basket over boiling water and steamed until just tender, a matter of minutes. Test for doneness by sticking the point of a small sharp knife into the thickest part. Toss the steamed potatoes with butter, olive oil or a seasoned oil, salt and pepper to taste, and any chopped fresh herb you like.

Baked potatoes can, all by themselves, be a lunch served with sour cream, crème fraîche, or crumbled fresh goat cheese, chopped fresh herbs, a shake of coarse salt and freshly cracked pepper, and, for those special occasions (which the Palmer family enjoys at the slightest suggestion), a heaping tablespoon or two of caviar! To bake Idaho (or russet) potatoes, preheat the oven to 400°F. Rub the well-washed potatoes with oil and randomly prick the skin with the tines of a kitchen fork. Place the potatoes on the center rack of the oven and bake for 45 minutes to 1 hour, or until a cake tester can be easily inserted into the center and is hot when pulled out.

Hash browns, made from leftover steamed or boiled potatoes, are a breakfast favorite at our house. For 6 people, you need at least 6 to 8 cooked large potatoes, cubed or shredded. Heat about 3 tablespoons clarified butter (see page 8), olive or vegetable oil, or bacon fat in a large heavy skillet (cast iron is best) over medium-high heat. Add the potatoes, $1/2$ teaspoon paprika, and salt and pepper to taste (maybe a diced half onion and/or some diced bell peppers). Press down on the potatoes with the back of a spatula to force them down into the hot oil, lower the heat, cover, and cook, checking the bottom for browning by lifting up an edge with the spatula from time to time, for about 20 minutes, or until the bottom is brown and crusty. Carefully turn the potatoes over in large pieces; don't worry if the pancake fulls apart. Cover and fry for an additional 10 minutes, or until browned on the second side. Serve hot.

No matter how many crisp oven-roasted potatoes I make for my family, there doesn't seem to be enough. Preheat the oven to 400°F. Quarter large potatoes (any kind of potato will do) or leave small ones whole. Peeling them or not is up to you. Place the potatoes in a roasting pan in a single layer and toss with olive oil to coat, chopped rosemary and/or thyme, and coarse salt and pepper. Roast the potatoes, turning them from time to time, for 30 to 45 minutes, or until cooked through, golden, and crisp.

And last, certainly not least, are mashed potatoes. I make my mashed potatoes by hand, pushing them through a ricer or food mill and then beating them with a potato masher or wooden spoon. If you prefer to go the electric mixer route, don't overbeat them, or the potatoes will be wet and starchy rather than smooth and fluffy. Remember, a few lumps won't hurt. I generally use russet potatoes, but any all-purpose potato will do. Add about 4 tablespoons (½ stick) butter and about ½ cup hot milk, half-and-half, or cream for every 2½ pounds of potatoes. You can also whip in a tablespoon or two of mashed roasted garlic (see page 6), some minced fresh flat-leaf parsley or chives, or ¼ cup grated or crumbled cheese after the potatoes are mashed. Use leftover mashed potatoes for potato cakes or as a casserole topping.

Roasted Beets and Garlic

Roasting beets intensifies their sweetness, and this is about as simple a dish as you can get. Once the beets go in the oven, they need no attention. They can be served hot or at room temperature, and any leftovers can go into salads. Use the smallest beets you can find.

SERVES 6

2 pounds small beets, about 1 inch in diameter

2 heads garlic, separated into cloves and peeled

2 tablespoons balsamic vinegar, or more to taste

Coarse salt and freshly ground black pepper

3 tablespoons olive oil

1. Preheat the oven to 350°F.

2. Trim the beets of their greens, leaving about a 1-inch top. Scrub them well. Combine the beets and garlic in a medium roasting pan and add ¾ cup water, the vinegar, and salt and pepper to taste.

3. Tightly cover the pan with aluminum foil and bake for about 45 minutes, or until the point of a small sharp knife can easily be inserted into the center of the beets. It is not necessary to do so, but if you want to remove the skins, working carefully, slip them off while the beets are still hot. Toss the beets and garlic with the olive oil. Taste and, if necessary, adjust the seasoning with additional vinegar, salt, and/or pepper.

Carrots in Guinness

We always have carrots on hand. They are a favorite snack for the boys. A quick sauté adds a nice extra vegetable at mealtime. But this preparation, made with Guinness stout and some maple syrup, imparts a rich, deep flavor to the common carrot. Use only fresh herbs; dried ones won't give the finished dish its necessary balance.

SERVES 6

3 tablespoons unsalted butter

1½ pounds carrots, peeled and cut diagonally into ¼-inch-thick slices

2 tablespoons minced shallots

1 cup Guinness stout

1 tablespoon minced fresh dill

1 tablespoon minced fresh flat-leaf parsley

1 tablespoon pure maple syrup

Coarse salt and freshly ground white pepper

1. Melt the butter in a large sauté pan over medium heat. Add the carrots and shallots and sauté for about 3 minutes, or until the carrots are nicely glazed.

2. Stir in the stout, dill, and parsley. Cover, lower the heat, and cook, stirring frequently, for about 8 minutes, or until the carrots are just barely tender. Stir in the maple syrup and salt and pepper to taste, raise the heat to high, and cook, uncovered, for about 5 minutes, or until all of the liquid has evaporated. Serve hot.

Grilled Asparagus and Spring Onions with Mustard Vinaigrette

Nothing simpler than vegetables straight off the grill tossed with a hint of vinaigrette dressing. Grilling brings out the sweetness of asparagus and adds a bit of smokiness to them. Spring onions, which I find in my city supermarket or at the farm stand down the road near the country house, are usually very mild, with just a gentle aroma of spice. A perfect combination. You can use almost any vinaigrette; balsamic or citrus also work well. And if you have some Parmesan cheese in the fridge, top the vegetables with a few shavings for an extra bit of tanginess.

SERVES 6

1 pound asparagus

1 pound very small spring onions (or scallions)

1 cup extra virgin olive oil

Coarse salt and freshly ground black pepper

2½ tablespoons red wine vinegar

1½ tablespoons Dijon mustard

1. Preheat the grill and oil the grill rack. Alternatively, preheat the oven to 500°F.

2. Break the tough ends from the asparagus. Using a vegetable peeler, peel the thicker skin from the stalks. Set aside on a platter.

3. Trim the roots, any damaged outside layers, and the excess green from the spring onions. You want the onions

to be about the same length as the asparagus. Add the onions to the asparagus.

4. Sprinkle ¼ cup of the olive oil over the vegetables, season to taste with salt and pepper, and toss to coat well.

5. Whisk together the red wine vinegar and mustard in a small bowl. Whisk in the remaining ¾ cup olive oil and season to taste with salt and pepper.

6. Place the asparagus and onions on the grill or on a baking sheet in the oven and grill or roast, turning frequently, for about 8 minutes, or until crisp-tender and nicely caramelized. Using tongs to keep from breaking them, return the vegetables to the platter. Give the vinaigrette a quick whisk and drizzle it over the hot vegetables. Taste and adjust the seasoning with salt and pepper. Serve warm.

Corn on the Cob Three Ways

Is there anything better than summer's first corn? Just-picked corn from a local farm stand is the mainstay of many of the Palmer house summer weekend meals. I cook it one of three ways, but I always make extra for corn cakes (a breakfast favorite), salads, or soups. In our family, lots of butter, salt, and pepper is usually all that fresh sweet corn needs, but corn dipped in Tabasco-seasoned melted butter with a squeeze of lime juice for a Southwestern flavor is also a favorite.

1. *To boil corn,* fill the biggest pot you own with cold water. Add 1 tablespoon sea salt for each gallon of water and bring to a boil. Add as many shucked ears as will easily fit in the pot and return the water to a boil. Immediately cover the pot and turn off the heat. Allow the corn to steep for 10 minutes. Using tongs, remove the corn from the water and serve.

2. *To grill corn,* carefully pull back some of the husk from each ear and remove the silk from the corn. Fold the husks back over to seal the corn. Place the corn in a pot with cold water to cover and allow to soak for 30 minutes.

3. Preheat the grill. Remove the corn from the water and shake off any excess. Place the wet corn on the grill and cook, turning frequently, for about 20 minutes, or until the corn kernels are tender but the husks are not blackened. Using an oven mitt, carefully remove the husks from the ears and serve. (You can also use this method to roast corn in a preheated 375°F oven.)

4. *To roast corn,* preheat the oven to 450°F. Shuck the corn and generously coat it with butter, salt, and pepper (or an herb- or spice-flavored butter). Tightly wrap each ear in aluminum foil and roast for 10 minutes, or until the corn is tender. Leave the ears wrapped in the foil and serve immediately.

Corn Pudding with Chanterelles and Shaved Parmesan

Corn pudding. My grandmother made it, my mother made it, and now I make it—in my restaurants and at home. This rather fancy version can be made plain and simple by eliminating the chanterelles, or you can use button mushrooms in their place—less expensive and tasty. Corn pudding, particularly if the corn is very sweet, lends itself to the addition of savory ingredients—minced fresh herbs, chiles and bell peppers, finely diced smoky meats, even smoked fish.

For a dinner party, bake the pudding in individual 6-ounce ramekins and serve with a fresh herb garnish. This rich, filling dish could be a main course for supper, served with a tossed salad of crisp lettuces and whatever vegetables you have in the refrigerator, some fresh bread, and, always, a glass of white wine for the grown-ups.

SERVES 6

2 tablespoons plus 2 teaspoons unsalted butter

1/2 cup minced (about 2 ounces whole) chanterelles

1 1/2 teaspoons fresh thyme leaves

8 ears corn, shucked

2 large eggs, separated

1/2 cup half-and-half

2 tablespoons butter, melted

1/3 cup Wondra flour

1/2 teaspoon freshly grated nutmeg

Pinch of cayenne pepper

Coarse salt and freshly ground black pepper

¾ pound chanterelles, trimmed and brushed clean

2 shallots, minced

¾ cup chicken broth

½ pound Parmesan cheese, in one piece

1. Preheat the oven to 400°F. Lightly butter a 2-quart deep casserole. Set aside.

2. Melt 2 tablespoons of the butter in a medium sauté pan over medium heat. Add the minced chanterelles and ½ teaspoon of the thyme leaves and sauté for about 4 minutes, or until the mushrooms are quite soft and have exuded most of their liquid. Remove from the heat and set aside.

3. Using a sharp knife, cut the kernels from each ear of corn, standing the cob upright on a cutting board and slicing downward. Then, one at a time, place the cobs on a plate and, using a small spoon, scrape out any remaining corn as well as its milk or scrape into a bowl. Measure out 3 cups of kernels; reserve the remaining kernels separately. Place the 3 cups corn and the corn scrapings and milk in a blender or food processor and process until very smooth.

4. Combine the corn puree, egg yolks, half-and-half, melted butter, sautéed chanterelles, and reserved corn kernels in a large bowl. Whisk in the flour, nutmeg, cayenne, and salt and pepper to taste.

5. Using an electric mixer, beat the egg whites until soft peaks form. Gently fold the egg whites into the corn mixture, taking care not to overmix. Spoon the mixture into the prepared casserole.

6. Place the casserole in a baking dish large enough to allow 1 inch of space all around the sides. Pour in enough hot water to come halfway up the sides of the casserole. Carefully place the dish in the oven and bake for about 45 minutes, or until the pudding is golden, set in the center, and nicely puffed.

7. While the pudding is baking, prepare the chanterelles. If they are large, slice them lengthwise in half. Melt the remaining 2 teaspoons butter in a large sauté pan over medium heat. Add the shallots and the remaining 1 teaspoon thyme and sauté for 2 minutes. Stir in the chanterelles and sauté for 3 minutes. Add the broth and salt and pepper to taste, lower the heat, and cook, stirring occasionally,

for about 5 minutes, or until the mushrooms are well cooked and slightly silky. Keep warm.

8. To serve, run a small sharp knife around the casserole and carefully unmold the pudding onto a serving plate. Spoon some of the chanterelles onto the center of the pudding and spoon the remaining mushrooms around the edge. Using a cheese shaver or the slicing side of a box grater, shave 6 to 8 slices of Parmesan cheese over the plate. (It's easier to get nice slices from a large piece of cheese; save the unused Parmesan for another recipe.) Serve immediately.

Sautéed Brussels Sprouts with Pancetta

People either love or hate brussels sprouts. But I've seen confirmed haters convert to lovers with this very simple recipe. Sautéing the individual leaves rather than the whole heads brings out their sweet flavor. Even my kids love this.

SERVES 6

1 pound brussels sprouts

¾ cup finely diced pancetta (see Note)

1 cup sliced shallots

1 teaspoon fresh thyme leaves

Coarse salt and freshly ground black pepper

1. Wash the brussels sprouts well. Cut out the small cores and carefully pull off the leaves. If the center leaves won't pull apart, slice them very fine. Set aside.

2. Place the pancetta in a large nonstick sauté pan over medium heat. Fry, stirring frequently, for about 12 minutes, or until the pancetta is crisp and has rendered most of its fat. If there are more than 2 tablespoons of fat in the pan, pour off the excess.

3. Add the shallots to the pan and sauté for about 6 minutes, or until they begin to take on some color. Add the brussels sprouts and thyme and season with salt and pepper to taste. Sauté for about 4 minutes, or until the leaves are tender but still slightly crisp. Serve immediately.

NOTE: Pancetta, an unsmoked Italian bacon, is available from Italian markets, specialty food stores, and some supermarkets. If you can't locate it, you can substitute slab bacon that has been blanched in boiling water or fine-quality ham. If you use ham, sauté it in about 1 tablespoon of oil, as it will not release much fat.

Sautéed Greens with Red Wine Vinegar and Roasted Shallots

Roasted shallots add a whole new dimension of sugary-sweetness to quickly tossed warm, tart greens. This simple dish can be a side, a salad, or the base for grilled chicken or fish. Add a bit of vinaigrette and some chopped leftover ham or chicken for a tasty lunchtime salad. A sprinkle of chopped hard-boiled egg would also be a nice addition.

SERVES 6

1 pound shallots, trimmed

½ cup olive oil

Coarse salt and freshly ground black pepper

12 cups tart greens (spinach, kale, arugula, endive, beet, etc.), trimmed, well washed, and dried

3 tablespoons red wine vinegar

1. Preheat the oven to 375°F.

2. Toss the shallots with about ¼ cup of the olive oil and season generously with salt and pepper. Place the shallots on a small baking sheet and roast, turning occasionally, for about 20 minutes, or until tender when pierced with the tip of a small sharp knife. Remove from the oven and set aside.

3. Place the remaining olive oil in a large deep saucepan over medium heat. Add the greens and season to taste with salt and pepper. Cook, continually tossing the greens with tongs, as the bottom layer will wilt very quickly, until most of the

greens have begun to wilt (the time will depend upon the toughness of the greens—baby spinach, for example, will take just a minute or two, broccoli rabe will take about 7 minutes). Add the shallots and toss for an additional minute.

4. Transfer the greens to a serving bowl or platter, drizzle the vinegar over the top, and toss to coat. Serve warm.

Orange-Braised Fennel with Hazelnuts

When a vegetable is best known for being eaten raw in salads, we often forget that it can be just as good when cooked and served as a side dish. Fennel, like celery and cucumbers, is one of those vegetables. This braise brings out fennel's sweet, subdued licorice flavor and is an ideal base for grilled or roasted fish, poultry, or pork.

SERVES 6

6 large fennel bulbs, trimmed

2 tablespoons butter or olive oil

½ cup chopped shallots

1 teaspoon grated orange zest

¾ cup fresh orange juice, strained

¾ cup chicken broth

Coarse salt and freshly ground black pepper

1 cup chopped toasted hazelnuts

1. Cut each fennel stalk bulb into 6 wedges of equal size. Set aside.

2. Melt the butter in a large sauté pan over medium heat. Add the fennel and shallots and sauté for 4 minutes. Add the orange zest, orange juice, broth, and salt and pepper to taste and bring to a simmer. Lower the heat, cover, and cook, stirring from time to time, for 45 minutes, or until the fennel is meltingly tender. Remove from the heat and stir in the hazelnuts.

3. Serve hot or at room temperature.

Cider-Baked Winter Squash and Apples

My kids eat almost everything, but winter squash had never been a family favorite until I added apples and maple syrup. That seemed to do the trick. This dish is often requested, particularly for our holiday tables. Ideal for casual cooks, it can be put together ahead of time and even baked beforehand. Reheating doesn't hurt it at all. Plus, it tastes good cold.

SERVES 6

2 large butternut squash, peeled, seeded, and grated

3 cooking apples, cored, peeled, and grated

1 medium onion, grated

1 teaspoon minced fresh sage

Coarse salt and freshly ground black pepper

½ cup apple cider

¼ cup pure maple syrup, or to taste

4 tablespoons (½ stick) unsalted butter, melted

1. Preheat the oven to 350°F. Lightly butter a shallow 2-quart square baking dish. Set aside.

2. Combine the squash, apples, onion, sage, and salt and pepper to taste in a large bowl.

3. Combine the cider and syrup in a small bowl, stirring until well blended. Pour over the squash and toss to combine. Taste and add more maple syrup if the squash lacks the touch of sweetness that is necessary to round out the dish.

4. Pack the squash mixture into the prepared baking dish, making sure that you pour all of the liquid into the dish. Pour the melted butter over the top. Bake for 45 minutes, or until the top is golden brown and the edges are beginning to pull away from the dish. Remove from the oven and allow to rest for 5 minutes before cutting into squares and serving.

Summer Vegetable Minestrone
with Pesto (page 14)

Crispy Oysters and Citrus
Mayonnaise on a Bulkie (page 78)

Salmon Salad with
Baby Spinach, Pea Shoots,
and Artichokes (page 60)

Tomatoes Stuffed with Shrimp Salad

(page 58)

Frittata

(page 82)

Green Tomato Tart

(page 84)

Speidies

(page 100)

(From top to bottom)
Corn Pudding with Chanterelles and Shaved Parmesan (page 111), Roasted Beets and Garlic (page 106), Orange-Braised Fennel with Hazelnuts (page 118), and Sautéed Brussels Sprouts with Pancetta (page 114)

Super Macaroni and Cheese

(page 123)

Pappardelle with Rabbit Sauce

(page 132)

Chicken Fricassee with
Dumplings (page 147)

Stuffed Roasted Pork Loin
with Spicy Applesauce
(page 180)

Lamb Shanks with Tomato, Lentils,
and Olives (page 172)

Whole Roasted Striped Bass with
Tarragon and Shallots (page 193)

Apple "Pizza" with
Cider Sorbet (page 207)

Pineapple Upside-down
Cake (page 230)

Brownie–Ice Cream Sandwiches

(page 223)

Dried Fruit and Nut Stuffing

There are endless recipes for stuffings, or dressings, to serve with turkey, chicken, or other birds. What you call them seems to depend on whether you're from the North or the South. Whatever you call it, it is a good idea to master one recipe and then vary it occasionally to go with the rest of the meal. I often try a new stuffing as an accompaniment to a roast chicken before serving it up with the big bird on the big day. A side bowl of stuffing adds a festive touch to any Sunday dinner, even if it isn't a holiday.

MAKES ENOUGH FOR ONE 16- TO 20-POUND TURKEY

12 cups ¼-inch cubes dried white and/or whole wheat bread

8 tablespoons (1 stick) unsalted butter

1 cup diced onions

¼ cup diced celery

1 tablespoon minced fresh flat-leaf parsley

1½ cups diced dried apricots

½ cup golden raisins

Approximately 2 cups warm turkey stock (page 36), chicken broth, or water

1 tablespoon poultry seasoning, or to taste

1 teaspoon chopped fresh sage, or to taste

1 teaspoon chopped fresh thyme, or to taste

1 teaspoon chopped fresh marjoram, or to taste

Coarse salt and freshly ground black pepper

1 to 1½ cups toasted walnut or pecan pieces

1. If not stuffing a bird, preheat the oven to 375 °F. Lightly grease a large shallow baking dish (about 4 quarts) or casserole. Set aside.

2. Place the bread cubes in a large bowl.

3. Melt the butter in a large sauté pan over medium heat. Add the onions, celery, and parsley, lower the heat, and sauté for 10 minutes, or until the vegetables are very soft but not browned. Add the apricots and raisins and sauté for an additional 3 minutes. Add 1 cup of the stock, the poultry seasoning, sage, thyme, and marjoram and cook for 3 minutes. Pour the mixture over the bread cubes, tossing to combine well. Add salt and pepper to taste and enough of the remaining warm stock to make a moist but not wet mixture. Toss in the nuts.

4. Use the mixture to stuff a bird (see Note), or place in the prepared baking dish or casserole and bake for about 35 minutes, or until the top is crusty and the stuffing is hot in the center.

NOTE: Corn bread, or rye, pumpernickel, or pumpernickel-raisin breads can be used in place of or with the white and whole wheat bread. Cooked rice, wild rice, or other grains can replace all or part of the bread. You can replace the apricots and raisins with any other dried fruit—either a single fruit or a combination— or chopped raw apples or pears. Any nut, including roasted chestnuts, can be used in place of the walnuts or pecans.

To this basic stuffing, you can add: 1 cup chopped cooked poultry livers, 1½ cups crumbled cooked sausage meat, or 1½ cups raw oysters. If you use any of these, you might want to eliminate the fruit and nuts.

Never stuff poultry in advance of roasting—even if the bird is refrigerated, bacteria can form quickly. Always stuff poultry just before you are ready to roast it.

Super Macaroni and Cheese

This luscious macaroni and cheese bears no resemblance to school lunchroom fare. Some white wine and three cheeses give this make-ahead casserole a whole new range of flavors. Don't have the three cheeses suggested here? Then substitute whatever you like with impunity. Gruyère, farmhouse cheddar, Caerphilly, Gouda, and Brie are good choices. Your mac 'n' cheese might even be better.

SERVES 6

3 tablespoons canola oil

¼ cup minced shallots

¼ cup minced celery

2 tablespoons Wondra flour

1½ cups half-and-half, heated

½ cup dry white wine

1 cup mascarpone cheese

¾ cup grated sharp white cheddar cheese

½ cup grated Fontina cheese

1 pound elbow or tube macaroni, cooked and well drained

Tabasco sauce

Coarse salt

¼ cup freshly grated Parmesan cheese, optional

¾ cup fresh bread crumbs

1. Preheat the oven to 350°F. Generously grease a 2-quart casserole. Set aside.

2. Heat the oil in a large nonstick saucepan over medium heat. Add the shallots and celery and sauté for 5 minutes, or until the vegetables are very soft. Lower the heat and stir in the flour until well incorporated. Whisk in the hot half-and-half and then the wine. Cook, stirring constantly, for about 4 minutes, or until the mixture has begun to thicken. Remove from the heat and beat in the cheeses, stirring until they have melted into the sauce.

3. Stir in the macaroni and season to taste with Tabasco and salt. Pour the mixture into the prepared casserole.

4. If using the Parmesan, combine it with the bread crumbs in a small bowl. Sprinkle the bread crumb mixture (or the bread crumbs) over the macaroni. Bake for 15 minutes, or until the edges are bubbling and the top is golden. Serve hot.

NOTE: To lower the fat in this recipe, replace the half-and-half with 1½ cups nonfat milk plus ¼ cup nonfat yogurt and the cheeses with reduced-fat cheese. When lowering fat in a cheese-based recipe, you will often lose flavor, but flavor can be enhanced with the addition of finely minced fresh herbs or chile peppers or even a chile-based salsa.

Pasta and Risotto

Pastas and risottos are, for the most part, fairly easy to prepare although they can sometimes be a bit time-consuming. Combining seasonal vegetables with an interesting pasta shape and a few aromatics (garlic, leeks, onions) always lures Court, Randall, Eric, and Reed to the table and guarantees a nutritious, well-balanced meal in a bowl. In the summer, what could possibly be better than pasta with a fresh tomato sauce? My whole family is a fan of this easy yet delicious dish.

Tomato Sauce: A basic tomato sauce for pasta or grilled meats or poultry is easy to make using either fresh or canned plum tomatoes. Sauté about 1 tablespoon minced garlic (more or less depending on your taste) in 3 tablespoons olive oil. Add about 2½ pounds fresh tomatoes, peeled, seeded, and chopped, or two 28-ounce cans chopped canned plum tomatoes, with their juices. Season to taste with chopped fresh basil, salt, and pepper and simmer for about 15 minutes, or until the sauce is slightly thickened. If desired, you can add red pepper flakes to taste. Store, tightly covered and refrigerated, for up to 3 days, or freeze for up to 6 months.

Bow Ties Tossed with Asparagus and Pancetta

This easy-to-make dish has plenty going for it—great texture and plenty of fresh taste and bright flavors. Serve it hot or at room temperature, as a main course or as a salad. Moisten leftovers with a light dressing of olive oil and balsamic vinegar for the next day's lunch. To make this throughout the year, substitute a seasonally available crisp green vegetable such as broccoli rabe or cabbage.

SERVES 6

1½ pounds bow ties (farfalle) or other small pasta

⅓ cup olive oil

1 pound pancetta, finely diced (see Note)

1 tablespoon minced garlic

½ pound asparagus, peeled, trimmed, and cut diagonally into
    1-inch pieces

¼ cup finely diced red bell pepper

1 tablespoon minced fresh flat-leaf parsley

Coarse salt and freshly ground black pepper

½ cup freshly grated pecorino Romano cheese, optional

1. Cook the pasta in boiling salted water according to the package directions. Drain well, reserving ⅓ cup of the cooking water. Return the pasta and the ⅓ cup cooking water to the cooking pot.

2. While the pasta is cooking, heat the olive oil in a large sauté pan over medium heat. Add the pancetta and garlic and sauté for about 5 minutes, or until the pancetta is beginning to crisp. (Lower the heat if the garlic begins to burn.) Add the

asparagus and red pepper and sauté for an additional 5 minutes, or until the asparagus is crisp-tender. Remove from the heat.

3. Toss the vegetable mixture into the hot pasta, then toss in the parsley and season to taste with salt and pepper.

4. Serve hot, with pecorino cheese sprinkled over the top if desired.

NOTE: You can use any type of bacon or even ham if you can't find Italian pancetta. For a meatless meal, eliminate the pancetta entirely and increase the amount of asparagus.

Cappellini with Fresh Tomatoes and Basil

Best made in the summer when vine-ripened tomatoes have their deepest flavor. This is an easy recipe, perfect for a lazy cook. Make the sauce in the morning (double the sauce for another meal or to use on grilled meats or fish). At mealtime, make a salad, boil up a pot of pasta, and pour a glass of light red wine. Out of season, use well-drained canned San Marzano tomatoes (two to three 28-ounce cans) for a different, but quite full-bodied tomato taste.

SERVES 6

4 pounds very ripe tomatoes

3 tablespoons extra virgin olive oil

1 shallot, minced

6 to 12 garlic cloves, chopped (see Note)

1/3 cup chopped fresh basil

Coarse salt and freshly ground black pepper

1½ pounds dried cappellini

1. Peel, core, seed, and finely chop the tomatoes. Place the tomatoes in a fine sieve set in the sink or over a bowl and allow to drain for 10 minutes.

2. Heat the oil in a large sauté pan over medium heat. Add the shallot and garlic, remove the pan from the heat, and allow the shallot and garlic to infuse the warm oil for 10 minutes. Add the drained tomatoes and the basil to the pan and season to taste with salt and pepper. Allow the sauce to stand for at least 1 hour and up to 8 hours before serving.

3. When ready to serve, cook the cappellini in boiling salted water according to the package directions. Drain well, return to the cooking pot, and toss with about 1 cup of the sauce. Serve in shallow pasta bowls, with the remaining sauce spooned over the top.

NOTE: You can use as much or as little garlic as you like. We like a lot.

Linguine with Eggplant Ragù

So many eggplant varieties are now available, ranging from the tiny globe-shaped red, pale green, cream, or variegated Asian to the more familiar deep purple or creamy white teardrop-shaped fruit used in Mediterranean cooking. Buy very young eggplant with a thin skin; they lack the bitterness often associated with older fruit. It's the older and bigger eggplant that require salting before cooking to sweeten the flesh and leach out the bitterness.

Make bruschetta or crostini with any extra ragù. Grill or toast large or small pieces of bread, season with garlic and oil, and top with a smear of ragù. Or use it as a sauce with couscous or other grains.

SERVES 6

2 medium tender young eggplant

¼ cup olive oil

1 cup diced red onions

3 cloves garlic, chopped

4 cups (one 28-ounce can) chopped canned Italian plum tomatoes, with their juice

1 tablespoon tomato paste

1 tablespoon chopped fresh basil

1 teaspoon minced fresh oregano

1 tablespoon chopped capers

1 tablespoon balsamic vinegar

Coarse salt and freshly ground black pepper

1½ pounds dried linguine

¼ cup shredded fresh basil

Freshly grated Parmesan cheese for serving

1. Trim the eggplant. You should not have to peel young eggplant, but if the skin seems tough, do peel it off. Cut the eggplant into small cubes.

2. Heat the oil in a large sauté pan over medium heat. Add the onions and garlic and sauté for 4 minutes. Stir in the eggplant and continue to sauté for about 10 minutes, or until the eggplant is beginning to take on some color. If the vegetables begin to darken too quickly, lower the heat.

3. Stir in the tomatoes, tomato paste, chopped basil, oregano, and capers, raise the heat, and bring to a simmer. Lower the heat and simmer for 30 minutes, or until the ragù is very well blended and aromatic. Stir in the vinegar. Season to taste with salt and pepper.

4. Meanwhile, cook the linguine in boiling salted water according to the package directions. Drain well and return to the cooking pot.

5. Add about 2 cups of the ragù to the linguine and toss to mix well. Transfer the linguine to a large serving platter and pour enough of the remaining sauce over the top to nicely sauce the pasta (reserve any ragù for another use; see the headnote above). Sprinkle with the shredded basil and serve with grated cheese passed on the side.

Pappardelle with Rabbit Sauce

I first tasted pasta sauced with rabbit in Tuscany when I was learning about truffle hunting, an experience that has been somewhat dimmed in my memory by the amount of grappa required to face the dogs and the dark and cold on the early-morning search for the elusive fungi. I do, however, remember the aromas and tastes of the hearty meals that I enjoyed in the Italian countryside. This sauce is a marvelous choice for a relaxed cook because it only gets better as it mellows over a couple of days. Instead of pasta, try it with a bowl of polenta.

SERVES 6

1 cup all-purpose flour

Coarse salt and freshly ground black pepper

Two 2½-pound rabbits, cut into 6 or 8 pieces

¼ cup olive oil, or more as needed

1 cup chopped onions

¼ cup finely chopped carrots

¼ cup finely chopped celery

1 tablespoon minced garlic

½ cup dry red wine

1 cup chicken broth

One 28-ounce can chopped Italian plum tomatoes, with their juice

1 teaspoon tomato paste

2 tablespoons chopped fresh basil

1 teaspoon chopped fresh rosemary

½ teaspoon chopped fresh oregano

2 tablespoons chopped fresh flat-leaf parsley

1 pound dried pappardelle

Freshly ground Parmesan cheese for serving, optional

1. Combine the flour with salt and pepper to taste in a shallow dish.

2. Rinse the rabbit and pat it dry. Lightly dredge it in the seasoned flour and set aside.

3. Heat the oil in a Dutch oven over medium heat. Add the rabbit pieces, a few at a time, and sauté, turning occasionally, for about 10 minutes, or until nicely browned. You may have to use additional oil to brown all of the rabbit. Transfer the rabbit to a platter as it is browned.

4. When all of the rabbit has been browned, add the onions, carrots, celery, and garlic to the pot and sauté for about 5 minutes, or until the vegetables have softened and are beginning to color. Add the wine and cook, stirring constantly to release any browned bits from the bottom of the pot, for about 3 minutes, or until the wine has begun to evaporate.

5. Stir in the broth and bring to a boil. Immediately return the rabbit to the pot. Add the tomatoes, tomato paste, basil, rosemary, oregano, and salt and pepper to taste, raise the heat, and bring to a boil. Immediately lower the heat to a simmer. Cover and simmer for 1 hour, or until the rabbit is very tender.

6. Using a slotted spoon, lift the rabbit pieces from the sauce, leaving the sauce at a simmer. Carefully remove and discard the skin. With a fork remove the meat from the bones and return it to the sauce. (You can make the sauce to this point up to 3 days in advance, cover, and refrigerate. Reheat before continuing with the recipe. The sauce can also be frozen for up to 3 months.) Stir in the parsley and simmer for 5 minutes.

7. Meanwhile, cook the pappardelle in boiling salted water according to the package directions. Drain well and return it to the cooking pot.

8. Add about 2 cups of the rabbit sauce to the pasta and toss to coat. Pour the pappardelle into a large shallow dish and spoon about 6 cups of the sauce over the top. If desired, sprinkle with cheese. Serve with the remaining sauce passed on the side.

Wild Mushroom Risotto

My family likes this so much that mushroom risotto can always be found on the table at our Christmas dinner. The boys love it, it is easy to prepare, and it tastes heavenly. What more could you ask of a family meal? I usually make a huge batch so any leftovers can be reheated, in pancake form, for the boys' lunch. To do this, add 1 beaten egg to every 2 cups leftover risotto. Pour the rice mixture into a very hot nonstick pan, well coated with melted butter. Fry, turning once, for about 10 minutes. You can make one large pancake and cut it into wedges or make individual cakes, as I do, to prevent fights at the table, and sprinkle a little grated Parmesan cheese over the warm pancake(s).

SERVES 6

7 to 9 cups chicken or vegetable broth

3 tablespoons unsalted butter

½ cup minced onion

½ pound wild mushrooms, trimmed, brushed clean, and sliced

1 pound Arborio, Carnaroli, or other medium-grain rice (see Note)

½ cup dry white wine, optional

½ cup freshly grated Parmesan cheese, plus more for serving if desired

Coarse salt and freshly ground white pepper

1. Place the broth in a large saucepan over medium heat. Bring to a simmer, then lower the heat to keep the broth hot.

2. Melt the butter in a large heavy saucepan over medium heat. Add the onion and mushrooms and cook, stirring frequently, for about 6 minutes, or until they are beginning to

soften and the mushrooms are exuding their liquid. Stir in the rice and cook, stirring constantly, for about 5 minutes, or until the rice is glistening and opaque.

3. Stir in the wine, if using, and cook, stirring constantly, until the wine has been absorbed by the rice. Begin adding the broth, 1 cup at a time, stirring until it has been absorbed by the rice. Continue adding broth until the rice is creamy and tender but still al dente. Fold in the cheese. Season to taste with salt and pepper.

4. Serve warm in large shallow soup bowls, with additional cheese sprinkled over the top if desired.

NOTE: Never rinse rice that you will be using for risotto—washing will remove the starch required to create risotto's creaminess.

If you want to do a bit of the work in advance, cook the risotto using about half of the broth, or until the rice has begun to soften but is still quite firm. Remove from the heat and allow to cool slightly, then cover and refrigerate for up to 2 days. When ready to serve, return the risotto to a large heavy saucepan and continue cooking and adding hot broth as above.

Poultry and Game Birds

In this chapter, chicken takes center stage. I always try to use the freshest, preservative-free, farm-raised birds available, simply because they taste so much better. If at all possible, do try to locate a local purveyor of these flavorful birds. But nothing says that you can't use the supermarket variety if that is all that you have available. Even if I only need certain parts, I always begin with a whole chicken because it is much more economical. Any of the recipes can, however, be adapted to other birds—Cornish game hens or turkey parts are particularly well suited. Many of my recipes are long-time favorites—such as my Mom's Barbecued Chicken—but you will also find a couple of recipes that introduce contemporary cooking techniques and ingredients, perfect for casual entertaining.

Perfect Roast Chicken

All good cooks think that they know the secret for making the perfect roast chicken—roast it breast side down, baste it every fifteen minutes, soak it in a salt brine—are some of the tricks often suggested. I *know* that mine is the perfect roast chicken. My secret? Lemon juice. It seals in the meat juices and helps crisp and brown the skin. A chopped lemon in the cavity while the chicken roasts makes a savory condiment for the finished plate. Although this calls for one chicken, I always roast two at the same time because I can make so many meals from the leftovers: chicken salads (page 63) and sandwiches (page 63) from the meat and rich, flavorful chicken soups from the carcasses. The other secret? Buy a top-quality chicken, preferably free-range.

SERVES 6

One 6-pound roasting chicken

1 lemon

1 large onion, peeled (or 1 large lemon, orange, or apple)

1 sprig fresh rosemary, optional

Coarse salt and freshly ground black pepper

½ cup dry white wine or water

Optional Gravy

1 tablespoon cornstarch, dissolved in 1 tablespoon cold water

1 cup chicken broth, or more as needed

1. Preheat the oven to 450°F.

2. Rinse the chicken under cool running water. Drain well and pat dry. (Reserve the giblets for another use, if desired.)

3. Cut the lemon crosswise in half and squeeze the juice onto the chicken skin, rubbing it in as you squeeze and moistening all of the skin with juice. Place the onion into the cavity, along with the optional sprig of rosemary. Season the cavity with salt and pepper to taste. Fasten the neck skin under the chicken with a small skewer. Close the cavity with a skewer or by sewing closed with a trussing needle and thread. Fold the wing tips under the wings. Generously season the chicken all over with salt and pepper.

4. Place the chicken on a rack in a heavy roasting pan. Push the legs back against the body, but don't tie them together, as this would keep the meat from roasting evenly. Pour the wine into the pan and roast for 30 minutes. Lower the heat to 375°F and continue to roast for about 1 hour longer, or until the chicken skin is golden-brown and crisp, the thigh meat is soft to the touch, and an instant-read thermometer inserted into the thickest part of the breast reads 155°F. Remove the chicken from the oven and let it stand for about 5 minutes.

To carve a chicken: To remove the wings, slice off at the joint next to the body. Set aside. Pull each leg slightly away from the body. Slice down through the thigh joint to remove the entire leg from the body. Slice through the leg joint to divide the drumstick and thigh. With the knife parallel to the breastbone, slice the breast meat away from each side of the carcass by cutting from the center of the breast slightly to the front, removing the meat in thin slices. Alternatively, remove the entire breast by carefully cutting it away from the breastbone and then cut the breast meat crosswise into thin slices. If desired, you can remove the skin from the chicken breast before slicing.

5. Meanwhile, if you want to make gravy, spoon off the excess fat from the roasting pan, after removing the chicken and rack. Place the pan on the top of the stove over medium heat. (This may require two burners.) Stir the cornstarch mixture and broth into the pan juices. Bring to a boil and cook, stirring constantly, for about 5 minutes, or until the gravy is smooth and the starchy taste has cooked out. Taste and adjust the seasoning with salt and pepper.

6. Carve the chicken and serve with the optional gravy on the side.

NOTE: Turkey can be roasted (12 to 15 minutes per pound or until an instant-read thermometer inserted into the thigh reads 175°F) using this same method. However, if you plan to make gravy, cook the giblets and neck in water (or chicken broth) to cover until tender. Remove the giblets and neck from the cooking liquid and strain it through a fine sieve. Use this liquid rather than chicken broth to make gravy as above. If desired, chop the meat from the giblets and neck and add it to the gravy.

If you want to stuff the turkey (try Dried Fruit and Nut Stuffing, page 121), do so just before roasting to prevent bacteria from developing or bake the stuffing separately, as I do.

Honey-Smoked Turkey

My backyard smoker makes summer entertaining so easy. Early in the morning, I season the poultry or meat, bank up my fire, wet down some aromatic wood chips (cedar, mesquite, hickory, apple, or pear), and follow the manufacturer's directions for method and time, from time to time taking a peek at the fire. When it's time for dinner, a perfectly smoked bird or roast is ready for the table. This recipe requires soaking the bird in a citrus-herb brine for at least 8 hours, or up to 24 hours, so plan ahead.

SERVES 6 PLUS, WITH LEFTOVERS

1 cup fresh orange juice

½ cup fresh lemon juice

3½ cups lavender-scented honey (or any flavor you like)

2 heads Roasted Garlic (page 6), pulp only

2 tablespoons fresh lavender leaves, optional

1 tablespoon fresh thyme leaves

1 tablespoon chopped fresh sage

1½ cups coarse salt

½ cup peppercorns

One 20-pound turkey, rinsed and patted dry

¼ cup grapeseed, canola, or other neutral vegetable oil

1. In a stockpot, lobster pot, or clean plastic tub large enough to hold the turkey, combine the orange juice, lemon juice, and 3 cups of the honey, mixing until very well blended. Stir in the roasted garlic, the optional lavender, the thyme, and sage, then stir in 1½ gallons (24 cups) ice water and the salt, mix-

ing until the salt begins to dissolve. Add the turkey. Cover and refrigerate for at least 8 hours but no more than 24 hours.

2. Prepare your smoker according to the manufacturer's directions for smoking a 20-pound turkey.

3. Combine the oil with the remaining ½ cup honey, mixing until well blended. Remove the turkey from the brine and pat it dry. Rub the outside of the bird with the oil-honey mixture. Place the turkey in the smoker and smoke according to the manufacturer's directions.

Mom's Barbecued Chicken

Whenever the Palmer family gathers in the summertime, my mom's barbecued chicken will be on the menu. Although my mother was much loved for her hospitality and well known for her zest for living, she wasn't much of a cook—except for her chicken. Everybody asked for her secret recipe, which she would never share. Now that my mom is no longer with us, my sister, Brenda, is the keeper of the recipe and it is usually her contribution to any family party. The leftovers, if you are lucky enough to have any, make great chicken salad.

SERVES 6

Two 3½-pound chickens, cut into serving pieces, rinsed, and
    patted dry

2 large eggs

1 cup Wesson Right Blend oil (see Note)

1 tablespoon coarse salt, or to taste

1 tablespoon Bell's poultry seasoning

1 teaspoon freshly ground black pepper

2 cups cider vinegar

1. Place the chicken in a shallow glass baking dish large enough to hold it in two layers or less.

2. Combine the eggs with the oil in a medium bowl, whisking until very well blended. Whisk in the salt, poultry seasoning, and pepper, then whisk in the vinegar. Pour the mixture over the chicken. Cover with plastic wrap and refrig-

erate for at least 8 hours but no more than 24 hours, turning the chicken from time to time to ensure that each piece is well marinated.

3. When ready to cook, preheat the grill. You will want a very low heat.

4. Remove the chicken from the marinade. Grill, turning frequently and brushing with the marinade, for about 20 minutes, or until the juices run clear when the meat is pierced with the tip of a small sharp knife. If the skin begins to blacken before the chicken is cooked, lower the heat if you are using a gas grill or, if using a wood or charcoal grill, remove the chicken and allow the fire to die down before returning the chicken to the grill. (If all else fails, place the chicken in a preheated 375°F oven to finish cooking.) Serve hot off the grill or at room temperature.

NOTE: My sister insists that if you use this oil, you will have almost no fat flare-ups as you grill. I've tried it and I have to admit that she's right, but I can't tell you why this is so.

Baked Lemon Chicken

Simple yet so delicious. Always make more than you need for one meal; leftovers make a superb chicken salad. Lots of warm garlic bread is absolutely essential to sop up the lemon-scented cooking juices, to wrap around a warm piece of meat, and to wipe the plate clean. A Saturday night family favorite with piles of garlic bread, a bowl of slightly cheesy orzo or rice, and a big salad of romaine.

SERVES 6

Three 2- to 2½-pound broiling chickens, cut into serving pieces, rinsed, and patted dry

1 teaspoon grated lemon zest

1 cup fresh lemon juice

½ cup chicken broth

½ cup olive oil

3 tablespoons minced garlic

Coarse salt and freshly ground black pepper

½ cup chopped fresh flat-leaf parsley

1. Preheat the oven to 400°F.

2. Place the chicken pieces skin side up in a shallow baking dish large enough to hold them without crowding.

3. Combine the lemon zest, juice, broth, oil, and garlic in a medium bowl. Pour the mixture over the chicken. Season to taste with salt and pepper.

4. Bake the chicken, turning occasionally, for about 45 minutes, or until the juices run clear and the skin is golden and

crisp. If the skin is not as crisp as you would like, raise the oven temperature to broil and place the chicken under the broiler for about 10 minutes, or until it has reached the crispness you desire.

5. Transfer the chicken to a platter. Stir the parsley into the cooking juices and pour the juices over the chicken. Serve hot.

Chicken Fricassee with Dumplings

A tough old bird or stewing hen traditionally used for fricassee or soup is getting harder and harder to find, but a good butcher might help you out. If you are lucky enough to be able to obtain one from a local farmer, the cooking time should be increased by about 45 minutes. This is a wonderful old-fashioned dish that almost nobody makes anymore. It's so filling and full of rich goodness, and it makes the house smell like Grandma is in the kitchen. A perfect meal for a chilly fall family dinner. Unfortunately, we never have any leftovers.

SERVES 6

One 6-pound stewing hen, cut into serving pieces, or 6 pounds chicken parts, rinsed and patted dry

½ cup diced onion

2 celery stalks, sliced

1 large carrot, sliced

3 tablespoons minced fresh flat-leaf parsley

1 teaspoon minced fresh thyme

Pinch of saffron threads

2 cups chicken broth

½ cup dry white wine

Coarse salt and freshly ground black pepper

2 cups all-purpose flour

1 tablespoon baking powder

¼ cup solid vegetable shortening or lard or 4 tablespoons (½ stick) butter

1 large egg, beaten

Approximately 1 cup milk

1 tablespoon cornstarch, dissolved in 1 tablespoon cold water, optional

1. Place the chicken pieces in a Dutch oven or large heavy pot and add the onion, celery, carrot, parsley, thyme, and saffron threads. Pour in the chicken broth and wine and season with salt and pepper to taste. Add cold water to cover by about 1 inch, place over medium heat, and bring to a boil. Cover, lower the heat to a simmer, and simmer for 45 minutes, or until the chicken is very tender. Remove from the heat.

2. Using a slotted spoon, lift the chicken pieces from the cooking liquid and place them on a large platter. Cover loosely with foil to keep warm.

3. Strain the cooking liquid through a fine sieve back into the Dutch oven, discarding all of the solids. Bring to a boil over high heat.

4. Meanwhile, combine the flour, baking powder, and salt to taste in a medium bowl. Cut in the shortening to make a crumbly mixture. Stir in the egg and just enough milk to make a soft dough.

5. Drop the dumpling dough into the bubbling cooking broth by the heaping tablespoonful (use a wet tablespoon to keep the dough from sticking). Lower the heat to a gentle simmer, cover, and simmer for 15 minutes without removing the cover. Remove from the heat.

6. Meanwhile, carefully remove and discard the skin and bones from the hot chicken, keeping the meat in pieces that are as large as possible. Place the meat in the center of the platter and tent loosely with the foil to keep warm.

7. Using a slotted spoon, carefully lift the dumplings from the broth and place them around the chicken on the platter. Generously cover the chicken and dumplings with the cooking broth, which should be as thick as a gravy. (If the broth is not thick enough to serve as gravy, whisk in the optional cornstarch mixture over medium heat until thickened.) Pass the remaining gravy at the table.

Turkey Hash

What to do with leftover turkey—besides next-day sandwiches and the proverbial soup—has always been a post-holiday dilemma. Turkey hash is the answer at our house. It is so simple to prepare and so delicious. You can add leftover diced beets for red flannel turkey hash, make a stick-to-your-ribs variation with a cup or two of leftover stuffing, or top it with the traditional poached egg. Your family will never know that they are eating leftovers.

SERVES 6

3 tablespoons olive oil

1½ cups shredded cooked potatoes

1 cup finely chopped onions

¼ cup finely chopped red bell pepper

1 head Roasted Garlic (page 6), pulp only

1 teaspoon minced fresh thyme

1 teaspoon minced fresh sage

4 cups chopped cooked turkey

1 to 1½ cups leftover turkey gravy (see page 140)

1. Preheat the oven to 375°F.

2. Heat the oil in a heavy ovenproof frying pan (cast iron is great) over medium heat. Add the potatoes, onions, and bell pepper and sauté for about 5 minutes, or until the potatoes are beginning to take on some color and the onions and bell

pepper are very soft. Stir in the roasted garlic, thyme, and sage and sauté for another minute. Add the turkey and enough gravy to moisten nicely and stir until well combined.

3. Using a spatula, pack the hash down into the pan. Place in the preheated oven and bake for 20 minutes, or until the bottom is brown and the top is nicely crusted. Remove from the oven and allow to rest for 5 minutes.

4. Cut into wedges and serve.

Breast of Duck with Citrus Sauce and Mixed Fruit Chutney

This, for sure, is a "company's coming" kind of dish. If making it for just my family, I'd probably marinate the duck breasts in a rich red wine or citrus marinade and throw them on the grill. But every once in a while, I like to "cook fancy" for guests on my night off from the restaurant. Since the chutney can be prepared at least a week ahead of time and the sauce a day or two in advance, there's not much to do at party time. I often serve this dish with some cinnamon-scented couscous or mashed sweet potatoes, along with my favorite Sautéed Greens (page 116) on the side.

SERVES 6

2 pounds duck bones (see Note)

1 cup dry white wine

½ cup coarsely chopped carrots

½ cup coarsely chopped celery

½ cup coarsely chopped shallots

1 tablespoon minced fresh flat-leaf parsley

1 teaspoon minced fresh ginger

2 bay leaves

3 tablespoons Cointreau or other orange-flavored liqueur

2 cups chicken broth

2 cups orange juice

Coarse salt and freshly ground black pepper

6 large boneless duck breasts, skin on

1 teaspoon minced fresh chives

½ teaspoon grated orange zest

2 tablespoons unsalted butter

Mixed Fruit Chutney (recipe follows)

1. Preheat the oven to 375°F.

2. Using a cleaver or a chef's knife, cut the bones into 2-inch pieces. Place them in a small roasting pan and roast, stirring occasionally, for 30 minutes, or until well browned.

3. Remove the pan from the oven and place it on the stove top over medium heat. Add ½ cup of the wine and cook, stirring constantly to release the browned bits on the bottom of the pan, for 3 minutes, or until the liquid has almost evaporated. Scrape the bones and liquid into a large saucepan. Add the carrots, celery, shallots, parsley, ginger, and bay leaves and sauté for 4 minutes. Stir in the remaining ½ cup wine and the Cointreau and bring to a boil. Add the chicken broth, orange juice, and salt and pepper to taste and again bring to a boil. Lower the heat and simmer for about 40 minutes, or until the liquid has reduced to 1½ cups. Remove from the heat and strain the sauce through a fine sieve into a small saucepan; discard the solids.

4. Score the skin of the duck breasts into a crosshatch pattern, cutting down into but not through the skin. Season both sides with salt and pepper to taste. Heat a large heavy sauté pan over medium heat. When very hot but not smoking, add the duck breasts, skin side down, and cook, draining off the excess fat from time to time, for 14 minutes, or until most of the fat has been rendered out and the skin is nicely browned and crisp. (You may have to turn down the heat to keep the skin from burning.) Turn and cook for an additional 3 minutes, or until the meat is cooked to medium (155°F on an instant-read thermometer).

5. Just before the duck is ready, place the sauce over medium heat. Add the chives and orange zest and bring to a simmer. Whisk in the butter until well incorporated. Taste and adjust the seasoning with salt and pepper. Lower the heat and keep the sauce warm.

6. Using a very sharp knife, cut the duck breasts on the bias into thin slices. Fan each breast over couscous or mashed sweet potatoes, if desired, and spoon the sauce over the top. Garnish each serving with a scoop of chutney.

NOTE: I suggest you purchase whole ducks, boning out the breasts for use in this recipe. Use the legs for a stew or confit and the bones to make the citrus sauce.

Mixed Fruit Chutney

MAKES ABOUT 3½ CUPS

2 cups diced mixed dried fruit (such as apples, pears, mangoes, peaches, and cherries)
½ cup cider vinegar
3 tablespoons fresh orange juice
¼ cup packed light brown sugar, or to taste (see Note)
¼ cup granulated sugar, or to taste (see Note)
¼ cup chopped lemon pulp
¼ cup chopped orange pulp
¼ cup chopped red onion
1 teaspoon minced garlic
1 teaspoon minced fresh ginger
¼ teaspoon minced hot green chile
¼ cup golden raisins
1 tablespoon minced crystallized ginger
½ teaspoon ground cinnamon
⅛ teaspoon ground coriander

1. Place the dried fruit in a heatproof container and add boiling water to cover by 2 inches. Allow to sit for 1 hour, or until the fruit is nicely plumped. Drain well.

2. Combine the vinegar, orange juice, sugars, lemon, orange, onion, garlic, fresh ginger, and chile in a heavy saucepan over medium heat. Bring to a boil. Boil, stirring constantly, for about 2 minutes or until the sugar has dissolved. Stir in the drained dried fruit, the raisins, crystallized ginger, cinnamon, and coriander and

bring to a boil. Lower the heat and just barely simmer, stirring frequently, for 20 minutes, or until the mixture is quite thick. Remove from the heat and pour into a nonreactive container. Allow to cool to room temperature, then cover and refrigerate. (The chutney will keep for up to 3 months.)

NOTE: The amount of sugar required will depend upon the tartness of the dried fruit. About halfway through the cooking time, taste the chutney. If it seems too tart, add a bit more brown or granulated sugar.

Grilled Marinated Quail with Apple-Corn Relish

In the restaurant world, you get to work with and meet people from all over the world. In the kitchen, everyone from the busboys to the seasoned chefs can have input into new recipes, as we all want to learn about new ingredients, techniques, and flavors. I guess this is how the ever-popular idea of fusion cooking was born.

Here we have a recipe learned in my kitchen. It is based on a traditional Indonesian method of cooking chicken, but almost any poultry, game, or meat can be prepared in this fashion. The meat is grilled, then cooked on top of the stove, and then returned to the grill. If you are fortunate enough to have a grill insert in your kitchen stove, this is very easy to do. If not, and it's too cold to grill outside, try one of the small, inexpensive stove-top grills now widely available.

The accompanying relish—which is not essential but does add another interesting dimension to the dish—can be made year-round with frozen corn as it's the smoky taste of the corn rather than the sweetness of just-picked summer's fresh that makes the flavors come together.

SERVES 6

12 quail

Juice of 2 lemons

1 tablespoon tamarind pulp, dissolved in 2 tablespoons warm water (see Note)

1 cup canned unsweetened coconut milk (see Note)

¼ cup minced red onion

½ jalapeño chile, or to taste, stemmed, seeded, and minced

1 tablespoon minced garlic

Coarse salt

Apple-Corn Relish (recipe follows)

1. Preheat the grill and oil the grill rack.

2. Split the quail lengthwise in half. Rub them all over with the lemon juice. Set aside.

3. Strain the tamarind liquid through a fine sieve; press against the sieve. Combine the tamarind liquid, coconut milk, onion, chile, garlic, and salt to taste in the blender and process until very smooth. Set aside.

4. Place the quail on the grill and grill for 2 minutes per side. Remove the quail from the grill (but do not turn off the grill). Using a cleaver or a heavy frying pan, lightly pound each quail half to flatten it slightly. Place the quail in batches, if necessary, in a large heavy nonstick frying pan over medium-high heat, pour the tamarind sauce over the quail, and cook, stirring frequently, for about 6 minutes, or until the quail have absorbed most of the sauce. (The quail can be prepared up to this point early in the day and refrigerated.)

5. Brush the skin side of the quail with any remaining sauce and place on the hot grill, skin side down. Grill for about 3 minutes, or until the skin has crisped. Do not overcook, or the birds will be dry. Serve hot or at room temperature, with the relish.

NOTE: Tamarind pulp and coconut milk are now available at many supermarkets and certainly at almost all specialty food stores. However, if you have trouble locating the tamarind, you can replace it with 2 teaspoons fresh lime juice mixed with 1 teaspoon molasses. The flavor won't be quite the same, but it will still be delicious.

Apple-Corn Relish

MAKES ABOUT 3 CUPS

2 cups fresh corn kernels

1 cup finely diced Granny Smith apples

½ cup finely diced red onion,

1 clove Roasted Garlic (page 6), peeled and mashed

1 tablespoon olive oil

1 tablespoon rice wine vinegar

2 teaspoons apple cider or juice or 1 teaspoon pomegranate molasses (see Note)

Coarse salt and freshly ground black pepper

¼ cup toasted pine nuts

1. Place the corn kernels in a large nonstick sauté pan over high heat and cook, stirring constantly, for about 5 minutes, or until the kernels are a bit dry, smoky-tasting, and nicely colored. Scrape the corn into a medium bowl.

2. Add the apples, onion, and garlic and toss to combine. Stir in the oil, vinegar, and cider. Season to taste with salt and pepper. Just before serving at room temperature, toss in the pine nuts.

NOTE: Pomegranate molasses is available at Middle Eastern markets and some specialty food stores. It has a marvelous citrus tang that really brings out the flavors of the other ingredients in sauces, stews, chutneys, relishes—in fact, almost anything. It's inexpensive, a little goes a long way, and I recommend that you add it to your pantry.

Meat and Game

I'm a meat fan. As I've said so many times, I grew up in a meat-and-potatoes household, and these favorites remain the main feature at my table. My wife, Lisa, who is much more health conscious than I am, prefers that the whole family limit our cholesterol and saturated fat intake, but when I have the time to cook at home, I still put my heart and soul into the meat preparation. I let Lisa watch our health when I'm not at the controls.

Fortunately, my cooking is often done on weekends at our house in Long Island, where grilling is an easy casual way for me to get meat and game on the table. A well-prepared grilled steak, venison chop, or burger is absolutely what I look forward to.

Once in a while, roast up a crackling, juicy standing rib roast, make a succulent (and great as leftovers) pot roast, glaze a beautiful ham, or serve a warming plate of braised lamb shanks. When you dig in, you'll know that you are treating yourself very well.

Flank Steak with Grilled Vegetables

Flank steak is often called London broil, which is, in fact, a method of preparing meat, not a particular cut. And, since flank steak is most often marinated, broiled or grilled, and sliced on the bias into thin pieces, it qualifies as a London broil. All this to say that you can use any meat labeled London broil for this recipe. Any which way, I didn't want you to be confused. This is a very simple grill, with, if you're lucky, lots of good leftovers for salads or sandwiches.

SERVES 6

1 pound asparagus, trimmed

3 heads radicchio, washed, dried, and quartered

3 portobello mushrooms, stems removed and wiped clean

2 red bell peppers, cored, seeded, and cut lengthwise into sixths

2 large red onions, cut crosswise into ¼-inch-thick slices

1 large eggplant, trimmed and cut into ½-inch-thick slices

1¼ cups balsamic vinegar

1¼ cups olive oil

1 tablespoon plus 1 teaspoon minced garlic

1 tablespoon minced fresh thyme

Coarse salt and freshly ground black pepper

Two 2- to 2½-pound flank steaks

1 tablespoon paprika

1. Peel the lower stalks of the asparagus and place it on a large platter. Add the radicchio, mushrooms, peppers, onions, and eggplant to the platter. Pour 1 cup each of the vinegar

and oil over the vegetables and sprinkle with 1 teaspoon of the garlic, 1 teaspoon of the thyme, and salt and pepper to taste. Using your hands, gently toss the vegetables to coat them well. Set aside for at least 2 hours to marinate.

2. Meanwhile, wipe the flank steaks dry with a clean kitchen towel. Sprinkle the paprika over both sides and rub it in. Place the steaks in a shallow baking dish large enough to hold them without crowding. Combine the remaining ¼ cup vinegar, ¼ cup olive oil, 1 tablespoon garlic, and 2 teaspoons thyme and rub the mixture into both sides of the steaks. Cover with plastic wrap and allow to marinate at room temperature for 1 hour.

3. Preheat the grill and oil the grill rack.

4. In batches, grill the vegetables until crisp-tender, using tongs to turn them frequently. Each type will take a different amount of time, depending upon its thickness and the heat of the grill. As the vegetables are grilled, return them to the platter so that they can continue to absorb the marinade. When all of the vegetables are grilled, adjust the seasoning with salt and pepper.

5. Wipe the grill rack clean and oil it again. Remove the steaks from the marinade and grill, turning occasionally, for about 10 minutes for rare or 14 minutes for medium. Transfer the steaks to a carving board and let rest for 5 minutes.

6. Slice the steaks on the bias into thin strips, catching as much of the juices as you can and place on a platter. Pour the juices over the top. Serve immediately, with the grilled vegetables on the side. You might also want to grill some slices of peasant bread, as the grilled vegetables and steak with the marinade and juices make absolutely delicious open-faced sandwiches.

Perfect Pot Roast

What better smell to fill the house on a snowy day than the rich aroma of a simmering pot roast? I admit that I make pot roast so we can have the leftovers to make open-faced sandwiches. You can make the pot roast on one day, strain the liquid, and put it all back in the pot, then add the vegetables and finish cooking it the next. And you can have the leftovers throughout the week.

SERVES 6

2 tablespoons canola oil

One 6-pound beef rump roast

1 cup beef broth

1 cup dry red wine

2 large carrots, peeled, and coarsely chopped

1 large onion, coarsely chopped

2 tablespoons tomato paste

2 sprigs fresh marjoram

2 sprigs fresh thyme

2 bay leaves

Pinch of ground cinnamon

Coarse salt and freshly ground black pepper

18 to 24 pearl onions, peeled

18 baby carrots, peeled and trimmed

18 tiny new potatoes, scrubbed

12 baby turnips, scrubbed and trimmed

1 cup frozen petit peas, thawed and drained

1 tablespoon cornstarch, dissolved in 1 tablespoon cold water, or 1 tablespoon unsalted
   butter, softened, kneaded into 1 tablespoon all-purpose flour, optional

1. Heat the oil in a Dutch oven over medium heat. Add the meat and sear, turning frequently, until all sides are lightly browned. Remove the meat from the pot. Drain off all the fat from the pot and carefully wipe the pot clean with paper towels.

2. Return the meat to the pot, add the broth, wine, 1 cup water, the chopped carrots and onion, the tomato paste, marjoram, thyme, bay leaves, cinnamon, and salt and pepper to taste, and bring to a boil. Immediately lower the heat, cover, and cook at a low simmer for about 2 hours, or until the meat is almost tender.

3. Remove the meat from the cooking liquid and set it aside. Skim off the excess fat from the cooking liquid and strain the liquid through a fine sieve, pressing against the solids to extract as much of the liquid as possible. Discard the solids.

4. Return the meat and the strained liquid to the Dutch oven. Add the pearl onions, baby carrots, new potatoes, and turnips, place over medium heat, and bring to a boil. Lower the heat and simmer for 15 minutes. Add the peas and cook for an additional 5 minutes, or until the vegetables are tender.

5. Remove the meat and vegetables from the cooking liquid and place them on a serving platter. Tent lightly with aluminum foil to keep warm.

6. If the cooking liquid is not as thick as you would like for gravy, return it to medium heat and whisk in the optional cornstarch mixture or the butter-flour mixture a small amount at a time, until the gravy is as thick as you would like.

7. Slice the meat into ¼-inch-thick pieces and arrange it down the center of the serving platter. Place the vegetables around the edge of the platter and spoon some gravy over the top. Serve with the remaining gravy passed on the side.

Roast Beef with Yorkshire Pudding

In these days of extreme health-conscious dining, not many people sit down to a huge, fat-crackling, well-seasoned roast beast, as my boys call it. To me, there is nothing more traditional or homier. It is a treat and should be treated like one. I know that I don't have to tell you that there is no waste; leftover roast beef makes the best sandwiches and salads or a great hash, and you can even, if there is enough meat left on them, devil up the bones with a bit of mustard and bread crumbs and heat them up for a pregame snack.

SERVES 6 TO 8

One 4-rib standing beef rib roast

½ teaspoon coarse salt plus more to taste

Freshly cracked black pepper

Yorkshire Pudding

1½ cups all-purpose flour

¼ teaspoon baking powder

¼ teaspoon sugar

1¼ cups milk

2 large eggs

3 tablespoons cornstarch or Wondra flour

2 cups beef broth or water

1. Preheat the oven to 500°F.

2. Generously coat the roast with salt and cracked pepper.

Place it fat side up on a rack in a roasting pan and roast for 30 minutes. Lower the heat to 375°F and roast for about 15 minutes per pound for rare, 18 minutes per pound for medium, or 22 minutes per pound for well-done (or until an instant-read thermometer inserted into the thickest part reads 140°F for rare, 155°F for medium, or 170°F for well-done).

3. Thirty minutes before the roast is done, combine the all-purpose flour, baking powder, and sugar with ½ teaspoon salt in the bowl of a food processor. With the motor running, add the milk and eggs and process until smooth. Let rest for 30 minutes.

4. Remove the roast from the oven. Place it on a carving board or platter and let it stand for 15 minutes before carving. Raise the oven temperature to 425°F.

5. Spoon 3 tablespoons of the pan drippings from the roast into an 8 × 11-inch baking dish. Place the pan in the oven for 2 minutes, or until it is very hot. Remove from the oven and immediately pour in the Yorkshire pudding batter. Bake for 15 minutes, or until the pudding has pulled away from the sides of the pan, has puffed up, and is golden brown.

6. While the pudding is baking, drain off all but 3 tablespoons of fat from the roasting pan. Place the roasting pan over medium heat on top of the stove (this might require two burners). Whisk in the cornstarch until well incorporated. Whisk in the beef broth and cook, stirring constantly, for about 5 minutes, or until the gravy has thickened and the starchy taste has cooked out. Taste and adjust the seasoning with salt and ground pepper. Remove from the heat.

7. Carve the roast (see Note). Cut the Yorkshire pudding into squares and serve hot with the roast beef, passing the gravy on the side.

NOTE: To carve a standing rib roast, lay the roast on its side. Using a long sharp carving knife, slice the meat away from the backbone and ribs in one piece. Stand the meat up and, holding it steady with a carving fork, slice into thin slices, cutting down across the grain.

If you want to make Yorkshire Pudding without roast beef, substitute 3 tablespoons unsalted butter for the pan drippings. The batter can also be used to make 12 popovers, baked as directed above.

Sage-Seasoned Roast Loin of Veal
with Melted Leeks

A loin of veal is what my Mom would call "a very fancy cut of meat." It is quite expensive, but there is no substitute for it and it is worth every penny because the meat is so tender and delicious. If you're expecting dinner guests, the meat can be prepared well in advance of roasting and the leeks can be cooked and reheated just before serving. Use leftovers, if you're lucky to have any to make swell Reuben-like sandwiches, with the leeks replacing the sauerkraut.

SERVES 6

2 shallots, minced

2 large white mushrooms, trimmed, brushed clean, and minced

¼ cup chopped fresh sage

2 tablespoons chopped fresh flat-leaf parsley

1 tablespoon chopped fresh chives

¼ teaspoon ground nutmeg, or to taste

¼ to ⅓ cup olive oil

Coarse salt and freshly ground black pepper

One 5- to 6-pound loin of veal, trimmed of excess fat

Approximately 1 pound very lean bacon

12 large leeks

3 tablespoons unsalted butter

1 cup chicken broth

1 teaspoon grated orange zest

1. Combine the shallots, mushrooms, sage, parsley, chives, and nutmeg. Stir in enough of the oil, a tablespoon at a time, to make a thick paste. Season to taste with salt and pepper. Smooth the mixture over the veal. Wrap the bacon around the roast to cover it completely, using kitchen twine to tie the bacon in place. Tightly wrap the roast in heavy-duty aluminum foil and refrigerate for 8 hours.

2. About 1 hour before cooking, remove the roast from the refrigerator and allow it to come to room temperature. (Do not unwrap.)

3. Preheat the oven to 400°F.

4. Place the wrapped roast in a heavy roasting pan and roast for about 2 hours, or until an instant-read thermometer reads 140°F for rare or 150°F for medium. Remove the roast from the oven and place it on a platter. Carefully unwrap the roast and discard the foil.

5. While the veal is roasting, prepare the leeks. Trim the leeks of most of the green part and the root ends. Cut lengthwise in half. Wash well under cold running water to remove all the grit, drain well, and pat dry.

6. Combine 1 tablespoon of the remaining oil with the butter in a large heavy sauté pan over medium heat. Add the leeks and season to taste with salt and pepper. Add the broth and orange zest and bring to a simmer. Cover, lower the heat, and cook, barely simmering, for about 1 hour, or until the leeks are meltingly tender. Transfer to a serving platter.

7. Carve the veal roast and arrange on a bed of the leeks, spooning the meat juices over the top.

Leg of Lamb with Spring Vegetables

Lean, sweet spring lamb used to be available only in the springtime and was much anticipated after seasons of older, stronger-tasting meat. Due to changes in breeding and imported meat, spring lamb (five to seven months old) is now sold all year round, but only lamb sold from March through October can legally be labeled "genuine spring lamb." Much of the lamb that we buy today comes from New Zealand and is shipped to us frozen. However, New Zealand lamb is still pastured and fed with mother's milk and the quality of the meat is consistently good. Although the tiny new vegetables make this an ideal springtime meal, don't hesitate to make this dish throughout the year, using whatever root vegetables are in the market. Leftover lamb and vegetables can be turned into a hash, chopped for a sandwich filling, or simply enjoyed at room temperature.

SERVES 6

One 6- to 8- pound leg of spring lamb, trimmed of excess fat

10 small cloves garlic, peeled

1 tablespoon celery seeds

Coarse salt and cracked black pepper

2 pounds tiny new potatoes, scrubbed

1 pound tiny turnips, scrubbed and trimmed (see Note)

1 pound baby carrots, scrubbed and trimmed (see Note)

1 pound thin asparagus, trimmed (see Note)

1 pound spring onions, peeled

1 tablespoon olive oil

½ cup dry white wine

¼ cup chicken broth

1. Preheat the oven to 450°F.

2. Wipe the leg of lamb with a damp cloth. Randomly cut 10 small slits just large enough to hold a garlic clove into the meat. Insert a garlic clove into each slit. Generously coat the lamb with the celery seeds and salt and cracked pepper.

3. Place the lamb fat side up in a roasting pan and roast for 30 minutes. Lower the heat to 350°F and roast for about 1 hour longer, or until an instant-read thermometer reads 140°F for rare or 145° to 150°F for medium. (Leg of lamb usually requires about 15 minutes per pound for a nice pink interior.)

4. While the lamb is roasting, prepare the vegetables: Place the potatoes in a medium saucepan with salted water to cover and bring to a boil over high heat. Lower the heat and cook for 10 minutes, or until the potatoes are almost cooked through. Drain well and pat dry.

5. One at a time, blanch the turnips, carrots, and asparagus in a saucepan of boiling salted water just to set their color. Drain well and pat dry.

6. Place the vegetables, including the onions, on a platter and toss with the olive oil and salt and pepper to taste.

7. Thirty minutes before the lamb is ready, add the seasoned vegetables to the roasting pan, spooning some of the pan juices over them. Roast for 30 minutes, or until the vegetables are cooked through and beginning to caramelize.

8. Remove the pan from the oven, transfer the lamb and vegetables to a serving platter, and tent lightly with foil to keep warm. Allow the lamb to rest for about 10 minutes before carving.

9. Meanwhile, pour or spoon off any excess fat from the roasting pan. Place the roasting pan on top of the stove over high heat. (You may need to use two burners.) Add the white wine and bring to a boil. Boil rapidly for 3 minutes. Add the broth and continue to boil for another 3 to 5 minutes, or until the liquid has reduced slightly. Pour the sauce into a gravy boat.

10. Carve the lamb into thin slices and serve with the vegetables and sauce.

NOTE: Leave a bit of the green stems on the turnips and carrots. (Use real live tiny baby carrots with the tops intact.) Use pencil-slim new asparagus if you can find it.

Grilled Leg of Lamb with Herbs and Roasted Garlic

At our house, the first use of the grill after a long winter's nap is usually for a butterflied leg of lamb. The smokiness adds just the right flavor to the tender spring lamb. The secret to perfect succulent grilled rolled lamb is a very low steady heat coming off the coals. If the exterior of the meat is blackening before the interior has reached the proper temperature, remove it from the grill and finish roasting the lamb in a preheated 400°F oven.

I gather up lots of roasted garlic and fresh herbs to add real zest to the meat. The intensely flavored meat makes absolutely delicious sandwiches, piled high on grilled peasant bread with some roasted red peppers.

SERVES 6

1 cup dry red wine

1 cup olive oil

2 cloves garlic, chopped

3 tablespoons minced fresh flat-leaf parsley

1 teaspoon minced fresh rosemary

One 4- to 5-pound butterflied leg of spring lamb

3 heads Roasted Garlic (page 6), pulp only

2 tablespoons chopped fresh chives

2 tablespoons chopped fresh tarragon

2 tablespoons chopped fresh chervil

Coarse salt and freshly ground black pepper

1. Combine the red wine, ¾ cup of the olive oil, the chopped garlic, 1 tablespoon of the parsley, and the rosemary in a shallow glass baking dish large enough to hold the lamb. Lay the lamb in the dish and turn it several times to coat well. Cover with plastic wrap and refrigerate for at least 6 hours, or up to 24 hours, turning the meat occasionally.

2. Preheat the grill and oil the grill rack.

3. Combine the roasted garlic, chives, tarragon, chervil, the remaining ¼ cup olive oil, and the remaining 2 tablespoons parsley in a small bowl. Using a fork, mash the ingredients together.

4. Remove the lamb from the marinade and pat it dry with paper towels. Season both sides of the lamb with salt and pepper to taste. Spoon the roasted garlic mixture over the boned side of the lamb and use a wooden spoon to distribute it evenly over the meat. Roll the long side of the lamb up, jelly-roll fashion, and tie it in place using kitchen twine.

5. Place the lamb on the grill and grill, turning frequently, for about 45 minutes, or until an instant-read thermometer registers 140°F for rare or 145° to 150°F for medium. Remove from the grill and allow to rest for at least 10 minutes before carving thin slices. Serve hot or at room temperature.

Lamb Shanks with Tomato, Lentils, and Olives

Lamb or veal shanks make a magnificent braise. While cut-up veal shanks are used in the Italian osso buco, lamb shanks are not quite as well known. When braised with the classic flavors of Provence, the meat falls off the bone. If you make extra, this rich dish will see you through a couple of casual meals. If all of the meat is gone, use the liquid as a sauce for noodles, polenta, or rice.

SERVES 6

3 tablespoons olive oil

6 whole lamb shanks (about 1 pound each)

1 cup chopped red onions

1 tablespoon minced garlic

1 large carrot, peeled and chopped

1 celery stalk, chopped

1 cup dry red wine

1 teaspoon minced fresh rosemary

1 teaspoon minced fresh thyme

1 teaspoon minced fresh marjoram

1 teaspoon minced fresh basil

1 cup beef broth

1 to 2 cups chicken broth

2 cups chopped canned Italian plum tomatoes, with their juice

Coarse salt and freshly ground black pepper

2 cups green lentils, picked over, rinsed, and drained well

1 cup pitted Niçoise olives

1. Preheat the oven to 375°F.

2. Heat the oil in a Dutch oven over medium heat. Add the shanks and sear in batches, if necessary, turning frequently, until the meat is nicely browned on all sides. Remove the shanks from the pot and set aside.

3. Pour off all but 1 tablespoon of fat from the pot. Add the onions and garlic and sauté for 3 minutes. Add the carrot and celery and sauté for 4 minutes. Pour in the red wine, raise the heat to high, and cook, stirring constantly to release the browned bits in the bottom of the pot, for about 5 minutes, or until the wine has begun to evaporate.

4. Stir in the rosemary, thyme, marjoram, and basil. Add the beef broth and 1 cup of the chicken broth and stir to combine. Return the shanks to the pot and pour the tomatoes over the top. Season to taste with salt and pepper. Cover, place in the oven, and bake for 1½ hours.

5. Remove the pot from the oven and stir in the lentils and olives. If the cooking liquid seems very thick, stir in the remaining 1 cup chicken broth. Cover and bake for 30 minutes or longer, until the lentils are tender and the meat is almost falling off the bone. Serve with buttered noodles, polenta, or mashed potatoes (see page 105).

NOTE: If you have them on hand, artichoke hearts (frozen are fine) make a great addition to this braise. Add them when you add the lentils.

A Light Lamb Stew

Traditionally lamb stew is made with neck or shoulder meat on the bone. Although bones make a richer-tasting broth, I prefer very lean, boneless lamb stew meat. I combine the lean meat with a bit of broth, wine, and spring vegetables for a very light stew that my family loves on a chilly day.

SERVES 6

1 tablespoon canola oil

Coarse salt and freshly ground white pepper

2½ pounds boneless extra-lean lamb stew meat, cut into 1½-inch cubes

2 pounds tiny new potatoes, scrubbed

1 pound spring onions, trimmed

1 pound baby turnips, scrubbed and trimmed

1 pound baby carrots, scrubbed and trimmed

¼ cup minced fresh flat-leaf parsley

1 teaspoon minced fresh thyme

2 cups chicken broth or water

1 cup dry white wine

Juice of 1 lemon

1. Heat the oil in a large sauté pan over medium heat. Season the meat with salt and pepper. Add the lamb, in batches, to the hot oil and sauté, turning frequently, for about 5 minutes, or until nicely colored. Transfer the browned meat to paper towels to drain thoroughly, then place in a Dutch oven or a large flameproof casserole with a lid.

2. Add the potatoes, onions, turnips, carrots, parsley, and thyme to the Dutch oven, tossing to combine. Season to taste with salt and pepper and pour the broth and wine into the pot. Place over high heat and bring to a boil. Immediately lower the heat and simmer for about 1 hour, or until the meat and vegetables are very tender. Remove from the heat and stir in the lemon juice. Taste and, if necessary, adjust the seasoning with salt and pepper. Serve hot in shallow soup bowls, with some crusty bread to absorb the flavorful broth.

Two Kinds of Ham

Two kinds of ham show up at our table—northern-style and southern-style. I grew up with the northern style—a commercially prepared, precooked ham that takes just a little cooking and looks great with the classic pineapple-clove garnish. But I've come to love southern-style ham—a salty, country-cured (but usually uncooked) ham that takes quite a bit of preparation and has to be sliced paper-thin to really be enjoyed. Both styles create great casual meals, as they leave just as much in leftovers as they provide for the original meal. Sandwiches, omelets, frittatas, scalloped potatoes, salads—you name it, you can incorporate ham into it. And please, don't throw out the bone. Use it to make bean or pea soup.

SERVES 6 TO 10

One 10- to 12-pound country ham or one 10-pound precooked ham

Approximately ¼ cup cloves

1 cup Madeira

1 cup packed light brown sugar

2 teaspoons dry mustard

1 teaspoon ground cinnamon

½ teaspoon ground ginger

1½ cups fresh bread crumbs

2 cups apple cider

1. *For country ham:* Purveyors of traditional Smithfield, Virginia, or other country hams include their own instructions for preparation on the sack that encloses the ham. However, all country hams must be soaked for at least 12 hours in cold

water and then cooked in boiling water to cover for at least 20 minutes per pound. Allow the ham to cool in the cooking liquid, then drain it and proceed with the following baking instructions. (If the specific instructions given by the purveyor are substantially different from mine, though, do follow them to ensure proper cooking.)

2. For either country ham or commercially prepared ham, preheat the oven to 375°F.

3. Using a sharp knife, carefully cut away the excess fat from the ham, but do leave a thin covering of fat in place. Using a small paring knife, score the top of the ham in a crosshatch pattern. Insert a clove in the center of each crosshatch. Place the ham on a rack in a roasting pan large enough to hold it easily.

4. Combine the Madeira, brown sugar, mustard, cinnamon, and ginger in a small bowl, blending well. Generously coat the top of the ham with the mixture. Sprinkle the bread crumbs over the top and sides, pressing lightly to make them adhere. Pour the apple cider into the roasting pan. Roast for about 1 hour, or until the meat is hot in the center and the crust is golden brown. (To test the ham, poke a thin metal skewer into the thickest part; if it comes out hot to the touch, the ham is ready.)

5. *To carve a country ham:* The wrapping sack may give instructions for slicing and serving. If it does not, using a very sharp knife, cut the ham, going straight across the top, into very thin slices—you want almost prosciutto-thin slices.

6. *To carve a commercially precooked ham:* Make deep cuts at each end down toward the bone, then run the carving knife along the bone from end to end. Carve slices by cutting down to the bone against the grain.

7. Serve the ham hot or at room temperature, with plenty of tangy mustard. I especially like a seasoned mustard such as horseradish or spiced grainy mustard, but a good strong Dijon mustard is just fine.

NOTE: To take a shortcut to meal preparation, cut yams and tart apples (1 of each per person) into thick slices and place them in the roasting pan before putting the pan in the oven. They will absorb the cider and the cooking juices and be absolutely delicious. Make some coleslaw or Sautéed Greens (see page 116) to complete the meal.

Grilled Pork Tenderloin with Asian Marinade

Pork tenderloin is one of my favorite meats. Its mild flavor calls out for marinades, sauces, and rubs. It is tender and easy to prepare, and it can be enjoyed hot or cold. Asian flavors go well with pork; they accent the meat's mildness and add a hint of sweetness for contrast. The pungent rosemary adds an intense note to the Asian marinade. I use black sesame seeds for their color, texture, and nuttiness, but white sesame seeds can be substituted.

SERVES 6

Three ¾- to 1-pound pork tenderloins

½ cup soy sauce

½ cup dry sherry

½ cup honey

¼ cup rice wine vinegar

¼ cup vegetable oil

2 tablespoons fresh orange juice

¼ cup black sesame seeds

1½ tablespoons minced fresh rosemary

1 tablespoon minced shallots

1 teaspoon minced fresh ginger

1. Trim the tenderloins of all fat and silverskin. Place them in a shallow baking dish large enough to hold them without crowding.

2. Combine the soy sauce, sherry, honey, vinegar, oil, and orange juice in a medium bowl, whisking until well blended.

Stir in the sesame seeds, rosemary, shallots, and ginger. Pour the mixture over the tenderloins. Cover with plastic wrap and allow to marinate at room temperature for 2 hours.

3. Preheat the grill and oil the grill rack.

4. Remove the pork from the marinade, shaking off any excess. Place the tenderloins on the grill and cook, turning frequently, for about 18 minutes, or until an instant-read thermometer inserted into the thickest part reads 155°F. Transfer to a platter and allow the meat to rest for 10 minutes before carving. (The internal temperature will climb to 160°F while the meat rests.)

5. Meanwhile, place the marinade in a small saucepan over medium heat and bring to a simmer. Simmer for 10 minutes, or until slightly thickened.

6. Slice the pork into ¼-inch-thick slices, spoon the hot marinade over the pork, and serve. This dish is especially good with basmati rice or rice noodles, which can be seasoned with a bit of the hot marinade. The leftovers make a great lunch salad.

Stuffed Roasted Pork Loin with Spicy Applesauce

While there are more ingredients in this dish than in most in this book, much of the preparation—the stuffing and the sauce—can be done well ahead of time. You can butterfly the roast yourself or have the butcher do it for you. Stuff the roast in the early afternoon. Once the roast goes in the oven, prepare Sautéed Greens with Red Wine Vinegar and Roasted Shallots (page 116) or Sautéed Brussels Sprouts with Pancetta (page 114).

Thinly sliced leftover pork can be made into rustic sandwiches on rye bread, topped with some of the greens. Add some of the applesauce to jazz up the mayonnaise, or spread on some honey mustard.

SERVES 6 TO 8

3 tablespoons unsalted butter

½ cup minced shallots

2 cups diced peeled Granny Smith apples

¼ cup finely diced celery root

1 teaspoon minced fresh sage

¾ cup apple cider, or more if needed

2 cups mashed cooked butternut squash

½ cup toasted pistachios

1¼ teaspoons ground cinnamon, or more to taste

¼ teaspoon ground cardamom

2 cups dry corn bread crumbs

Coarse salt and freshly ground black pepper

1 head Roasted Garlic (page 6), pulp only

One 3- to 4-pound boneless pork loin roast

1 cup dry white wine

Spicy Applesauce (recipe follows)

1. Preheat the oven to 400°F.

2. Melt 1 tablespoon of the butter in a large sauté pan over medium-low heat. Add the shallots and sauté for 5 minutes, or until the shallots are quite soft but not brown. Add the apples, celery root, and sage and sauté for an additional 5 minutes. Add ½ cup of apple cider and cook for 2 minutes. Scrape the mixture into a large bowl.

3. Add the butternut squash, pistachios, 1 teaspoon of the cinnamon, and the cardamom and stir to combine. Stir in the corn bread crumbs and salt and pepper to taste, mixing until just combined. Taste and, if necessary, adjust the seasoning with salt and pepper and additional cinnamon. If the mixture is not moist, add additional cider by the teaspoonful until you achieve the consistency you desire.

4. Combine the roasted garlic with the remaining 1 teaspoon cinnamon and ¼ cup apple cider. Set aside.

5. Lay the pork fat side down on a cutting board. Starting at a long side, make a long, straight horizontal cut about halfway through the meat. Then cut up but not through each side to open up and butterfly the meat.

6. Spread about 1½ cups of the apple stuffing down the center of the butterflied pork. Fold the sides of the pork over the stuffing and pat the roast back into shape. Using kitchen twine, tie the roast in place.

7. Place the remaining stuffing in a lightly greased baking dish. Dot the remaining 2 tablespoons butter over the top. Cover and set aside.

8. Season the roast with salt and pepper to taste. Generously rub the roasted garlic mixture over the roast. Place the roast cut side down on a rack in a heavy roasting pan and pour the wine into the pan. Roast for 20 minutes. Reduce the heat to 350°F and roast for an additional 1 hour, or until an instant-read thermometer inserted into the thickest part reads 150°F. Remove the roast from the oven, tent lightly with aluminum foil, and allow it to rest for 10 minutes (the internal temperature will continue to rise as it rests) before slicing.

9. Meanwhile, 20 minutes before the roast is done, place the reserved stuffing in the oven. Bake for 20 minutes, or until just heated through.

10. Cut the meat into ¼-inch-thick slices. Serve on a bed of the stuffing, allowing 2 to 3 slices per serving, with the applesauce spooned over the top.

Spicy Applesauce

MAKES ABOUT 2 CUPS

2 tablespoons unsalted butter
2 Granny Smith apples, peeled, cored, and chopped
1 shallot, chopped
1 teaspoon minced fresh ginger
¼ teaspoon minced serrano chile, or to taste
¾ cup apple cider
¾ cup chicken broth
3 tablespoons Calvados or applejack brandy
Coarse salt and freshly ground black pepper

1. Melt the butter in a medium saucepan over medium-low heat. Add the apples, shallot, ginger, and chile and sauté for 5 minutes. Add the cider and broth and bring to a simmer. Simmer for 15 minutes, or until the apples are mushy and the liquid has reduced slightly. Remove from the heat and pour into a blender. Process until smooth.

2. Pass the applesauce through a fine sieve into a clean saucepan. Add the Calvados and season to taste with salt and pepper. Place the pan over medium heat and bring the sauce to a simmer. Simmer for 3 minutes, or just until the intensity of the alcohol has cooked off. Serve hot. (You can prepare the applesauce up to 3 days in advance. Cover and refrigerate, then reheat just before serving.)

NOTE: For wonderful flavor, when the applesauce is cooked, remove the excess fat from the juices in the pork roasting pan and add the pan juices to the sauce, then proceed as directed.

Venison Chops with Zinfandel Sauce and Caramelized Turnips

Venison chops are usually our last stab at the grill before the first snowfall, although I have been known to light up the grill in the middle of winter, standing in my khaki shorts as the temperature plunges. The sauce and the turnips can be made in advance. Just some grill time, a few minutes to caramelize the turnips in a pan, and dinner is ready. If you prefer a vegetable other than turnips, be my guest.

SERVES 6

2 pounds venison or beef bones, cracked (see Note)

1½ cups zinfandel

½ cup chopped carrots

½ cup chopped celery

½ cup chopped red onion

1 tablespoons minced fresh flat-leaf parsley

1 teaspoon dried thyme

2 bay leaves

½ cup dried cherries

2 cups chicken broth

2 cups beef broth

Coarse salt and freshly ground black pepper

Six 8-ounce venison chops, 1½ inches thick

2 tablespoons corn oil

1 teaspoon minced fresh thyme

2 tablespoons unsalted butter

Caramelized Turnips (recipe follows), optional

1. Preheat the oven to 375°F.

2. Place the bones in a small roasting pan and roast, stirring occasionally, for 30 minutes, or until well browned.

3. Remove the pan from the oven and place it on the stove top over medium heat. Add ½ cup of the wine and cook, stirring constantly to release the browned bits from the bottom of the pan, for 3 minutes, or until the liquid has almost evaporated. Scrape the bones and liquid into a large saucepan.

4. Add the carrots, celery, onion, parsley, dried thyme, and bay leaves and sauté for 4 minutes. Stir in the remaining 1 cup wine and the dried cherries and bring to a boil. Add the chicken and beef broths, along with salt and pepper to taste, and bring to a boil. Lower the heat and simmer for about 40 minutes, or until the liquid has been reduced to 1½ cups. Strain the sauce through a fine sieve into a small saucepan, discarding the solids.

5. Preheat the grill and oil the grill rack.

6. Rub the chops with the oil and season to taste with salt and pepper. Grill for 30 seconds, or just long enough for the grill to mark the meat. Then turn and grill for about 15 minutes, turning once or twice, or until the chops are medium-rare. Remove from the grill and set on a warm platter.

7. Reheat the sauce over medium heat. Add the fresh thyme and whisk in the butter. Taste and, if necessary, adjust the seasoning with salt and pepper.

8. Pour the sauce over the chops, add the turnips to the platter, if desired, and serve.

NOTE: You can either have the butcher crack the bones or use a cleaver at home.

Caramelized Turnips

SERVES 6

2 pounds tiny turnips with their greens
3 tablespoons unsalted butter
2 tablespoons pure maple syrup

½ cup chicken broth

Coarse salt and freshly ground black pepper

1. Scrub the turnips and trim them, leaving about ¾ inch of the greens. Place the turnips in a medium saucepan with cold water to cover and bring to a boil over high heat. Lower the heat and simmer for 5 minutes, or until the turnips are just barely tender. Remove from the heat and drain well.

2. Melt the butter in a large sauté pan over medium heat. Add the maple syrup and stir to incorporate, then whisk in the broth. Add the turnips and season to taste with salt and pepper. Bring to a boil, then lower the heat, cover, and cook, stirring frequently, for about 15 minutes, or until the turnips are nicely glazed and tender when pierced with the point of a small sharp knife. If the pan becomes too dry before the turnips are nicely glazed, add water, 1 tablespoon at a time. Serve hot.

Seafood

I'm an avid fisherman, so I am very aware of the difference between fresh fish and not-so-fresh fish. Also, I live in New York, where we have many fine-quality fish markets, staffed with knowledgeable personnel. If a supermarket is the only place you can buy fish, my advice is to befriend the person behind the seafood counter to ensure that you are purchasing truly fresh fish, or order fresh seafood by e-mail or telephone.

Fresh fish is firm but resilient when touched. It should have no fishy odor, but should faintly smell of fresh sea breezes. For whole fish, the scales should be intact, with a fine, gel-like coating. The eyes should be bright and almost alive-looking, while the gills should be bright red (or, at the least, florid pink). Smell the gill area or the stomach cavity of a whole fish; if there is any odor at all, don't buy it.

With the exception of the one for soft-shell crab, all of the recipes in this section can easily be adapted to whatever fish or shellfish you can purchase locally. It is far better to use the freshest seafood possible than to stick to the type given in a particular recipe if it is not absolutely fresh and delicious.

Whole Roasted Salmon with New Potatoes and Leeks

Fishing could easily fill my days—and nights. Wherever I go, I always try to get in some fishing—deep-sea, surf-casting, bonefishing, fly—you name it, I've tried my line at it.

While on a brief salmon fishing vacation on the Orcas Islands off the coast of Washington State, I fished all day. On the way home, I stopped at my host's garden to pick the accompaniments for the day's catch, keeping the ingredients simple so we could enjoy the clean, fresh ocean taste of the fish.

If you don't have a whole wild salmon (and how often do any of us have such a luxury?), use a farm-raised salmon or any other slightly fatty fish of the same weight. If you can't find a 6-pounder, there is no reason not to roast 6 (or as many as you need) smaller fish. If you don't like rosemary, use any herb or aromatic that you like or have on hand.

SERVES 6

1½ pounds new fingerling potatoes, scrubbed

One 6-pound salmon, cleaned, head and tail left on

Three 5-inch branches fresh rosemary

1 lemon (unpeeled), washed and sliced crosswise, plus 6 additional slices for garnish if desired

Coarse salt and freshly ground black pepper

¾ pound very thinly sliced premium smoky bacon

6 leeks (white part with a trace of green), split lengthwise and well washed

1 teaspoon fresh rosemary needles

Cracked black pepper

2 bunches watercress or arugula green, trimmed of tough stems and well washed, optional

1. Bring a large saucepan of salted water to a boil. Add the potatoes, reduce the heat, and simmer for about 5 minutes, or until just slightly cooked. Drain and pat dry. Set aside.

2. Preheat the oven to 375°F.

3. Rinse the salmon and pat it dry. Place the branches of rosemary into the cavity, then place the lemon slices on top of the rosemary. Season to taste with salt and pepper, keeping in mind that the bacon will add additional saltiness to the salmon. Carefully wrap the salmon in the bacon strips, completely covering the top.

4. Place the leeks and potatoes in a shallow roasting pan large enough to hold the salmon. Sprinkle the vegetables with the rosemary and season to taste with salt and pepper, again keeping in mind that the bacon will add saltiness. Lay the bacon-wrapped salmon on top of the vegetables. Sprinkle the top with cracked black pepper.

5. Roast for about 15 minutes per inch of thickness of the fish, or until an instant-read thermometer registers 135°F when inserted into the thickest part of the salmon. Remove the pan from the oven and allow to cool to room temperature, about 30 minutes.

6. Place the fish on a serving platter and surround it with the vegetables. If desired, garnish the platter with watercress and lemon slices. Serve at room temperature.

Salmon Cakes with Herbed Tartar Sauce

Quite a long way from my mother's salmon croquettes, these succulent little fish cakes can also be used as an hors d'oeuvre when formed into bite-sized pieces. Serve the sauce as a dip. No smoked salmon? Just use 1 pound fresh. The yellow bell pepper can be replaced with red or green, or even eliminated; the herbs can be a combination of any that you particularly like. Worried about cholesterol? Use 2 egg whites in place of the eggs called for. Don't like heat? Kill the chile. No Plochman's mustard? Substitute any fine-quality, slightly sweet mustard. Whatever you choose, you will welcome the fact that both the cakes and the sauce can be made well in advance of dinner.

SERVES 6

¾ pound salmon fillet, skin and any pinbones removed

¼ pound smoked salmon

1 large egg

1 large egg yolk

2 teaspoons Plochman's mustard

½ teaspoon Tabasco sauce, or to taste

½ teaspoon Worcestershire sauce, or to taste

2 teaspoons olive oil

½ cup minced red onion

¼ cup finely diced yellow bell pepper

1 teaspoon minced serrano chile, or to taste

1 cup fresh bread crumbs

¼ cup minced fresh flat-leaf parsley

2 tablespoons minced fresh chives

1 teaspoon minced fresh mint

2 tablespoons vegetable oil

Herbed Tartar Sauce (recipe follows)

1. Coarsely chop the fresh and smoked salmon together. Cover and refrigerate until ready to mix with the remaining ingredients.

2. Whisk together the egg, egg yolk, mustard, Tabasco, and Worcestershire sauce in a small bowl. Set aside.

3. Heat the olive oil in a large sauté pan over medium heat. Add the onion, bell pepper, and chile and sauté for about 4 minutes, or until the vegetables have just softened. Remove from the heat.

4. Place ½ cup of the bread crumbs in a medium bowl, add the sautéed vegetables and the reserved salmon mixture, and toss to combine. Stir in the egg mixture, along with the chopped herbs. Cover with plastic wrap and refrigerate for about 3 hours, or until the mixture is well chilled.

5. Place the remaining ½ cup bread crumbs on a plate or pie tin. Set aside.

6. Remove the salmon mixture from the refrigerator and form it into twelve 1-inch-thick cakes of equal size. (Before forming the cakes, you may want to take about a teaspoon of the mixture and fry it quickly in a bit of oil just to cook it through, so that you can adjust the seasoning to your taste; do not taste the raw mixture, as it has uncooked egg in it.) Roll each cake in the bread crumbs to coat and place on a baking sheet. (The salmon cakes can be made up to 24 hours in advance. Tightly wrap the salmon cakes in plastic wrap and refrigerate).

7. Heat the vegetable oil in a large nonstick frying pan over medium heat. Add the cakes, without crowding, in batches, if necessary, and cook, turning once, for about 6 minutes, or until golden on both sides and cooked through. Transfer the cakes to paper towels to drain. (The cakes can be cooked up to 4 hours ahead, covered and refrigerated. Reheat in a preheated 300°F oven for about 5 minutes, or until heated through.)

8. Serve hot, or at room temperature, with the tartar sauce on the side.

Herbed Tartar Sauce

MAKES ABOUT 2 CUPS

4 sweet gherkins, halved

3 shallots, halved

¼ cup pitted French or Italian green olives

1 tablespoon capers

3 tablespoons chopped fresh parsley

1 tablespoon chopped fresh tarragon

1 tablespoon chopped fresh dill

1 tablespoon chopped fresh chives

1 large hard-boiled egg yolk

1 cup mayonnaise

1 tablespoon Dijon mustard

1 tablespoon fresh orange juice

¼ cup sour cream

Coarse salt and freshly ground black pepper

Combine the gherkins, shallots, olives, capers, parsley, tarragon, dill, and chives in a food processor and process until coarsely chopped. Add the egg yolk, mayonnaise, mustard, and orange juice and pulse just until combined. Add the sour cream and salt and pepper to taste and process to just combine. Scrape the sauce into a bowl or other nonreactive container, cover, and refrigerate until ready to use. (The sauce can be made up to 3 days in advance.)

NOTE: Use any combination of herbs that you like. This is a great sauce for any grilled fish or shellfish or spread for fish or poultry sandwiches.

Whole Roasted Striped Bass with Tarragon and Shallots

Bass fishing is one of my favorite pastimes. I get out on the waters around Long Island whenever I can, and when I visit my family in central New York, I fish the rivers and streams. My older boys now like to join me and the thrill they feel when catching their own dinner makes me proud. If you don't fish, most fish markets will have some type of whole bass on hand, but if you can't find one, use thick fillets of any sweet white-meat fish such as halibut. Roasting fish at a high temperature seals in its juices so it stays extremely moist.

SERVES 6

Two 3-pound striped bass, cleaned

2 tablespoons olive oil

2 teaspoons fresh lemon juice

8 large fresh tarragon sprigs, plus additional sprigs for garnish if desired

Coarse salt and freshly ground black pepper

4 cups (about 2½ pounds) sliced shallots, blanched

1 teaspoon minced fresh tarragon

½ cup dry white wine

Lemon slices for garnish, optional

1. Preheat the oven to 450°F.

2. Rinse the fish and pat dry both inside and out. Combine the oil and lemon juice and generously rub the mixture over

the fish. Place 4 tarragon sprigs into the cavity of each fish. Season inside and out with salt and pepper to taste.

3. Combine the shallots and minced tarragon in a shallow roasting pan large enough to hold the fish and season to taste with salt and pepper. Pour the wine over the shallots and lay the fish on top.

4. Roast, occasionally stirring up the shallots, for about 30 minutes, or until the shallots are very tender and an instant-read thermometer inserted into the thickest part of the fish registers 135°F. Remove the pan from the oven and allow the fish to rest for 5 minutes.

5. Using two spatulas, carefully lift the fish to a serving platter. Spoon the shallot mixture around the fish. If desired, garnish the plate with additional tarragon sprigs and lemon slices.

Sautéed Soft-Shell Crabs with Brown Butter

What would spring on the East Coast be without soft-shell crabs? The soft-shell crab season seems to be getting longer and longer, but the crabs are at their best in April, when the waters are still cold. As the season lengthens, I find the shells too tough for my liking. For an informal meal, fry up some crabs and tuck them into warm, soft rolls with a little lemon-flavored mayonnaise and some chopped romaine lettuce.

SERVES 6

9 slices of home-style white bread, toasted

18 small soft-shell crabs, cleaned

1½ cups Wondra flour

Coarse salt and freshly ground black pepper

Approximately ½ cup canola oil or Clarified Butter (page 8)

½ pound (2 sticks) unsalted butter

Juice of 1 lemon

1 tablespoon minced fresh parsley

Lemon wedges for garnish, optional

1. Trim the crusts from the toast and discard (or save for bread crumbs). Cut each slice in half on the diagonal, making 18 triangles. Set aside.

2. Rinse the crabs and gently squeeze out any excess water. Pat very dry.

3. Place the Wondra on a plate and season it to taste with salt and pepper. One at a time, dip the crabs into the seasoned flour to lightly coat. Shake off the excess flour.

4. Heat about half the oil in a large sauté pan over medium heat until very hot but not smoking. Add a few of the crabs shell side down (you do not want to crowd the pan) and fry, turning once, for about 4 minutes, or until the crabs are golden brown and crisp and cooked through. (For safety, gently lay the crabs into the hot oil from the front to the back; this will send the splattering oil away from you rather than toward you.) Place the cooked crabs on a platter and continue frying until all of the crabs are cooked, adding additional oil as needed.

5. Pour off the oil from the pan, leaving any browned bits in the bottom of the pan. (If the bits of flour have turned black, wipe the pan clean.) Return the pan to medium heat and add the butter. Cook, allowing the butter to foam and then subside, for about 7 minutes, or until it has begun to turn golden brown and has a nutty aroma. Add the lemon juice and parsley and stir to combine. Remove from the heat.

6. Place 3 toast triangles on each plate. Lay a soft-shell crab on top of each toast, pour the brown butter over the top, and serve immediately, with a wedge or two of lemon on each plate, if desired.

Maryland Crab Cakes

The better the crabmeat, the better the crab cakes. Fresh crabmeat is available in the fish section of many supermarkets, so do look for it. Crab cakes can be shaped into any size, bite-sized for an hors d'oeuvre, or burger-sized to put on a crusty roll with tartar sauce, mustard-mayonnaise dressing, or coleslaw. The smaller ones cook in about half the time as the large ones.

SERVES 6

2 tablespoons (¼ stick) unsalted butter

2 tablespoons finely diced red bell pepper

2 tablespoons finely chopped scallions (including some green)

2 pounds fresh lump crabmeat, picked through for shells or cartilage

¾ cup fine-quality mayonnaise

2 tablespoons minced fresh flat-leaf parsley

1¼ cups fresh bread crumbs, toasted

Coarse salt

Tabasco sauce

¼ cup canola oil

1. Melt the butter in a medium sauté pan over medium heat. Add the bell pepper and scallions and sauté for about 6 minutes, or until very soft but not browned. Remove from the heat and set aside.

2. Combine the crabmeat, mayonnaise, and parsley in a mixing bowl. Scrape in the bell pepper and scallions and sprinkle

¼ cup of the bread crumbs over the top. Season to taste with salt and Tabasco and lightly toss together to just combine; do not overmix or compress the mixture. Shape the crabmeat mixture into 6 large cakes of equal size.

3. Spread the remaining 1 cup bread crumbs on a plate. Dip each crab cake into the bread crumbs, turning to coat all sides evenly. Place the coated cakes on a plate, cover loosely with plastic wrap, and refrigerate for up to 2 hours. (The cakes can be fried immediately, but they will not be as flavorful or as crispy as they will be if allowed to chill slightly.)

4. Heat the canola oil in a large sauté pan over medium heat. Add the crab cakes and fry, turning occasionally, for about 12 minutes, or until golden brown and heated through. If the coating begins to get too brown, lower the heat. Serve hot with lemon wedges, Herbed Tartar Sauce (page 192), or plain mayonnaise (or add some citrus juice and zest, minced herbs, garlic, or scallions to the mayo).

San Francisco Crab Boil

I travel frequently to San Francisco for business and just as often with my wife and kids for pleasure. Whatever the purpose, trying new restaurants and returning to new favorites is a given. I was introduced to the traditional San Francisco crab boil some years ago and took to it like a native. I'm usually lucky enough to be able to order West Coast Dungeness crabs through the restaurant. I usually allow 2 Dungeness crabs per person, but we're hearty eaters! To order Dungeness crabs from San Francisco, see page 235.

SERVES 6

6 lemon slices

6 lemons, cut into wedges

2 cups dry white wine

2 tablespoons crab boil seasoning (or seafood seasoning)

2 tablespoons coarse salt

1 tablespoon peppercorns

6 to 12 live Dungeness crabs

About 3 cups (1½ pounds) melted butter, or as much as you like

1. Since the proper way to eat crabs, which is best done outdoors, is an important part of the ritual, you must first prepare the table. Cover the picnic table with a good thick layer of newspaper. At each place setting, lay out a nutcracker, lobster cracker, hammer, or other tool that will help the diner crack the crab open; a pick to lift the meat from the shell; a bowl of water with a slice of lemon in it; a small bowl for melted butter; and a clean kitchen towel or large napkin to keep hands clean. Place bowl of lemon wedges, a basket of

sourdough bread, and a big salad (see page 40) in the center of the table. And set a tub holding lots of iced-down beer and white wine on the side.

2. Combine the wine, crab boil seasoning, salt, and peppercorns in a stockpot or lobster pot and add enough cold water to fill the pot about three-quarters full. Bring to a boil over high heat. Add the crabs, cover, and boil for about 20 minutes, or until the crabs are bright reddish orange. (If you really want to test for doneness, try pulling off a leg. If it comes off easily, the crab is cooked.)

3. Carefully lift the pot from the stove and drain off all the water. Place the pot in the middle of the table with a pair of tongs hanging from the side. Pour the melted butter into the dishes and dig in.

Pan-Roasted Lobster with Savory Rice Pilaf

Fresh lobster, quickly roasted to bring out its sweet tenderness, is nestled on a bed of warmly seasoned, aromatic basmati rice. In our house, lobster is not saved for company, it is just one of our favorite meals. Since almost every supermarket has a fresh lobster tank, you can make it one of yours also. Just make sure you pick lively lobsters that are feisty when removed from the tank. Any leftover lobster meat can be used for Lobster Club Sandwiches (page 74) or salads or stirred into a risotto near the end of the cooking time.

SERVES 6

¼ cup dried porcini mushrooms

¼ cup olive oil

1 tablespoon unsalted butter

¼ cup minced shallots

2 tablespoons minced celery

¼ teaspoon ground cumin

¼ teaspoon ground cardamom

1 cup basmati rice

½ cup millet or quinoa, well washed and drained

4 cups chicken broth

1 cinnamon stick

Coarse salt and freshly ground black pepper

Six 1½-pound live lobsters

Juice of 2 lemons

¼ cup chopped fresh flat-leaf parsley

1. Place the porcini in a small bowl, add boiling water to cover, and soak for 45 minutes. Drain well (discard the soaking liquid or strain it through cheesecloth and use it as part of the rice-cooking liquid). Chop the porcini and set them aside.

2. Preheat the oven to 500°F.

3. Heat 1 tablespoon of the olive oil with the butter in a large heavy saucepan over medium heat. Add the shallots and celery and sauté for 4 minutes, or until they are beginning to soften. Stir in the cumin and cardamom, along with the reserved porcini, until well blended. Stir in the rice and millet and cook, stirring frequently, for 2 minutes. Add the broth and cinnamon stick, raise the heat, and bring to a boil. Lower the heat to a bare simmer, cover, and cook for about 25 minutes, or until the rice and millet are tender. Remove from the heat and let rest for 5 minutes before serving.

4. Meanwhile: Here is the part most people hate, but somebody has to do it if you want to eat well. Kill the lobsters by plunging a very sharp chef's knife straight down into the cross just behind the head to kill the lobster instantly. Cut each lobster lengthwise in half, cutting down through the head and back and through the tail. Pull off the claws and set aside. Cut off and discard the head. Clean out the head sac and the intestines from the body.

5. Place the lobster pieces on two baking sheets with sides. Toss with the lemon juice, 3 tablespoons of the parsley, the remaining 3 tablespoon olive oil, and salt and pepper to taste. Roast for about 7 minutes, or until the flesh is just opaque and the shells are bright red orange, with a bit of brown along the cut edges.

6. Remove the cinnamon stick from the pilaf, add the remaining 1 tablespoon parsley, and fluff with a fork. Mound the pilaf on a serving platter and spoon the lobster over the top. Serve immediately.

Desserts

Although my restaurant Aureole is known for spectacular, take-your-breath-away desserts, I am just as comfortable with comforting, old-fashioned confections. My two favorite desserts in all of the world are My Favorite Chocolate Chip Cookies and Angel Food Cake with Raspberries and Cream—two very simple, "mom's kitchen" sweets.

Over the years, I have learned that there are two types of home cooks: Those who wow guests with the main course and those who wow them with dessert. When you focus on casual cooking and easy entertaining, though, you can do both, because most of my recipes do not require hours (or days) in the kitchen. Since I can't imagine any home-cooked meal without a dessert, I have gathered some of my favorite, easy-to-make finales.

Lemon Meringue Pie

This has been a Palmer family favorite for as long as I can remember. My grandmother made it, my mother made it—and so it goes. I have never heard anyone say that they didn't like lemon meringue pie and there are never, ever, any leftovers. So, if you want to have a slice for breakfast in the morning, bake two pies.

MAKES ONE 9-INCH PIE

Lemon Filling

1½ cups granulated sugar

2 tablespoons cornstarch

2 tablespoons sifted all-purpose flour

⅛ teaspoon salt

1 teaspoon grated lemon zest

Juice of 2 lemons

3 large egg yolks

4 tablespoons (½ stick) unsalted butter, cut into bits

1 teaspoon pure vanilla extract

One 9-inch Flaky Pie Pastry (recipe follows) shell, baked

Never-Fail Meringue

1 tablespoon cornstarch, dissolved in 1 tablespoon cold water

3 large egg whites

6 tablespoons superfine sugar (see Note)

1. Preheat the oven to 400°F.

2. Combine the granulated sugar, cornstarch, flour, and salt in a medium saucepan. Whisk in 1¾ cups cold water and cook, stirring constantly, for about 5 minutes, or until slightly thickened. Stir in the lemon zest and juice. Remove from the heat.

3. Place the egg yolks in a small bowl and gradually beat about ½ cup of the hot lemon mixture into them to temper them. Whisk the egg yolk mixture into the hot lemon mixture. Beat in the butter and vanilla and cook for an additional minute, or until the butter is well incorporated and the mixture is thick.

4. Pour the hot mixture into the baked pastry shell. Place ½ cup water in a small saucepan over high heat and bring to a boil. Whisk in the cornstarch mixture and cook, stirring constantly, for about 2 minutes, or until the mixture is clear. Remove from the heat and allow to cool.

5. Beat the egg whites in a large bowl with an electric mixer set at the lowest speed until just foamy. Increase the speed and continue to beat, alternately adding the cooled cornstarch mixture and the superfine sugar, until the whites are stiff and shiny.

6. Place most of the meringue on top of the center of the filling and put small spoonfuls of the remaining meringue around the edge of the filling. Using a large spatula, spread the meringue out from the center to meet the edge, making sure that the entire top is covered and the edge is sealed.

7. Bake for 10 minutes, or until the meringue is golden brown. Remove from the oven and allow to rest for about 15 minutes before cutting into wedges and serving. Refrigerate any leftovers.

Flaky Pie Pastry

MAKES ENOUGH FOR ONE 2-CRUST 9-INCH PIE

2 cups sifted all-purpose flour
¼ teaspoon salt
⅔ cup chilled solid vegetable shortening, lard, or a combination of shortening and
    unsalted butter

1. Combine the flour and salt in a food processor. Add the shortening and pulse until the mixture is crumbly. Add up to ¼ cup ice water, 1 tablespoon at a time, processing as you go, until the dough comes together in a loose ball; do not over-mix or let the dough get too wet.

2. Remove the dough from the processor, divide it in half, and shape each piece into a disk. Wrap each piece in plastic wrap and refrigerate for at least 15 minutes, or until chilled.

3. For a two-crust pie, on a lightly floured board, roll out each piece of dough to a circle about 12 inches in diameter and ⅛ inch thick. Fit one circle into a 9-inch pie pan, leaving the edges overhanging the pan. Fill the pan with the filling, then place the second circle of dough over the filling, pressing the edges of the pastry together with your thumb and forefinger. Trim off any excess pastry and crimp the edges together.

4. *For a one-crust pie,* roll out one piece of dough into a 10- to 12-inch circle and fit it into a 9-inch pie pan, leaving the edges overhanging the pan. Fold the excess dough under the edge. Using your thumb and forefinger, crimp a decorative edge. Using a fork, prick the bottom of the pie shell.

5. To prebake the crust, whisk together 1 large egg white and 1 tablespoon cold water. Using a pastry brush, lightly coat the pastry with this egg wash. Bake in a preheated 375°F oven for about 15 minutes, or until the crust is set and lightly browned.

NOTE: If you can't find superfine (or bar) sugar, process regular granulated sugar in a food processor or a blender until very fine. The meringue can also be used to make small crisp meringues to be filled with fresh fruit or pudding. Line a baking sheet with parchment paper. Place the meringue in a pastry bag fitted with a plain tip and create small baskets by piping a small circle (no more than 3 inches in diameter) for the bottom of each and then piping about three rings on top of each other around the outer edge. Bake in a very low oven (no more than 250°F) for about 2 hours, or until the meringue baskets are dry and crisp.

Apple "Pizza" with Cider Sorbet

My sister, Brenda, and her husband, Bill, run an old-fashioned cider mill in Fly Creek, New York, just outside Cooperstown. The mill's 1889 press, powered by a thumping waterwheel, makes a rich and delicious apple cider that has become a fixture on our fall table. After a day at the mill, it always seems natural to use the cider or just-picked apples in some part of the evening meal. Frequently, it is a main course of apples with pork or game. But if a vote were taken, an apple dessert would be my family's choice—and this one would be the favorite.

Although the pizza stands up well on its own, I like to give it yet another zap of apple with a scoop of cider sorbet. Because the sorbet is made with a puree of cooked apples rather than apple juice, it is creamy, not icy, and has a more substantial texture than most sorbets. But I'm sure a scoop of premium vanilla ice cream instead would bring no complaints.

MAKES ONE 8-INCH TART

3 medium Granny Smith apples (or Braeburn, pippin, or transparent)

Juice of 1 lemon

3 tablespoons apple cider

½ cup granulated sugar

3 tablespoons Wondra flour

1 tablespoon ground cinnamon

3 tablespoons unsalted butter, melted

½ recipe Flaky Pie Pastry (page 205)

2 tablespoons cinnamon sugar

Cider Sorbet (recipe follows)

1. Peel and core the apples. Halve them lengthwise and cut each half lengthwise into paper-thin slices. Place the slices in a medium bowl, sprinkle with the lemon juice, add the cider, and toss to combine. Add the granulated sugar, flour, and cinnamon and toss to coat well. Drizzle the melted butter over the top and toss again.

2. Preheat the oven to 375°F.

3. On a lightly floured surface, roll the dough, working from the center out, into a circle approximately 9 inches in diameter and ¼ inch thick. Carefully lift the dough onto an 8-inch pizza pan or a pizza stone. Fold the ½ inch of overhanging dough under itself all around to give the pastry circle a double thickness along the edge. Using your fingertips, crimp a neat fluted rim of dough.

4. Working from the edge toward the center, make concentric circles of slightly overlapping apple slices, with the outside edge of the slices toward the edge of the dough. In the center of the tart, use a few apple slices to make a slightly raised rosette shape. Sprinkle the apples with the cinnamon sugar.

5. Bake the tart for 40 minutes, or until the crust is golden and the apples are tender, caramelized, and beginning to brown on the edges. Remove from the oven and allow to cool for 15 minutes.

6. Cut the tart into wedges and serve with the sorbet.

Cider Sorbet

MAKES ABOUT 5 CUPS

2 pounds Granny Smith apples, peeled, cored, and finely chopped

1 cup apple cider or hard cider

1 cup sugar

1 cinnamon stick

1 teaspoon grated orange zest

½ cup fresh lemon juice

1. Combine the apples and ⅓ cup of the cider in a medium saucepan over medium heat. Bring to a boil, then reduce the heat to a low simmer and cook, stirring frequently, for 15 minutes, or until the apples have softened. Remove from the heat and allow to cool.

2. Stir the apples until blended into a smooth puree or puree in a blender or food processor.

3. Combine the sugar, 1 cup cold water, the cinnamon stick, and orange zest in a medium saucepan over medium heat, bring to a boil, and boil for 1 minute. Remove from the heat and add the lemon juice. Pour into a heat-resistant bowl, set in a larger bowl of ice water, and let stand until cold.

4. Strain the sugar syrup through a fine sieve; discard the cinnamon stick and zest.

5. Measure out 2½ cups of the apple puree and place in a bowl. Add the sugar syrup and the remaining ⅔ cup cider and stir to blend well. Pour the mixture into an ice cream maker and freeze according to the manufacturer's instructions for ice cream.

Chocolate–Chocolate Chip Cake

Who doesn't like chocolate, and who doesn't really like double chocolate? This simple cake is always a hit. My boys love it with a scoop of vanilla ice cream; I prefer dark coffee ice cream. With a bit of confectioners' sugar sprinkled over the top, the cake is a busy baker's dream, and it also freezes well, so you can plan ahead.

MAKES ONE 9-INCH CAKE

1 cup condensed milk

2 ounces unsweetened chocolate

8 tablespoons (1 stick) unsalted butter, softened

1½ cups granulated sugar

2 large eggs

1 teaspoon baking soda

1 cup milk

2½ cups sifted all-purpose flour

2 teaspoons pure vanilla extract

1½ cups semisweet chocolate chips

¼ cup confectioners' sugar

1. Preheat the oven to 350°F. Butter and flour a 9-inch springform tube pan. Set aside.

2. Combine the condensed milk and unsweetened chocolate in a small heavy saucepan over medium-low heat. Bring to a boil, stirring constantly, and cook, stirring constantly, for

about 5 minutes, or until the mixture resembles pudding. Remove from the heat and allow to cool.

3. Beat the butter and sugar in a large bowl with an electric mixer until light and fluffy. Add the eggs one at a time, beating until well incorporated. Add the cooled chocolate mixture and beat until well blended.

4. Add the baking soda to the milk in a small cup and stir until well combined. Beat the mixture into the batter. Sift the flour into the batter a bit at a time, mixing well. Stir in the vanilla. Fold in the chocolate bits, making sure that they are evenly distributed.

5. Pour the batter into the prepared pan. Bake for 45 minutes, or until the edges of the cake pull away from the pan and a cake tester inserted into the center comes out clean. (Some melted chocolate chips may appear on the tester but they will be shiny and chocolaty rather than looking like uncooked batter.) Cool in the pan on a wire rack for 15 minutes. Then remove the sides from the pan, invert onto a rack, and finish cooling on the rack.

6. To serve, place the confectioners' sugar in a small sieve and sift it over the top of the cake. Transfer the cake to a cake plate and serve.

Angel Food Cake with Raspberries and Cream

Although my restaurants are known for their elaborate desserts, no sweet can tempt me as much as a simple angel food cake. This classic has always been, and will remain, my birthday cake. Try leftover toasted angel food cake with a scoop of ice cream, or cubed, toasted, and tossed with slightly sweetened mixed berries for a dessert panzanella.

MAKES ONE 10-INCH CAKE

1 cup sifted cake flour

1½ cups sifted superfine sugar (see page 206)

1½ cups (about 13 large) egg whites, at room temperature

¼ teaspoon salt

1½ teaspoons cream of tartar

1 teaspoon pure vanilla extract

1½ cups chilled heavy cream, whipped

3 cups raspberries

A few sprigs fresh mint or mint leaves

1. Preheat the oven to 375°F.

2. Sift together the sifted cake flour with half of the sifted sugar at least three times.

3. Using an electric mixer, beat the egg whites and salt in a large bowl until very foamy. Sprinkle in the cream of tartar and add the vanilla and beat on high speed until soft peaks form. (This is very important. The peaks should hold, but not be firm and sharp.) Gradually sprinkle the remaining sugar

over the beaten egg whites, beating slowly to incorporate. On a slow speed, beat the flour-sugar mixture one-third at a time, scraping the sides and bottom of the bowl after each addition.

4. Immediately pour the batter into a sparkling-clean ungreased angel food cake pan with a removable bottom. Cut through the batter with a kitchen knife to burst any large air bubbles.

5. Bake for about 35 minutes, or until the cake has risen and is golden brown and a cake tester inserted into the center comes out clean. (Do not open the oven door for the first 20 minutes of baking or the cake may fall.) If the pan has feet, turn it upside down. If not, invert it over the neck of a heatproof bottle. Allow the cake to cool for at least 2 hours.

6. When the cake has cooled completely, turn it right side up and carefully run a sharp knife around the edges of the pan to release the cake. Lift the cake from the sides of the pan, holding onto the tube. Slowly and carefully run the knife around the center tube and then between the cake and the pan bottom. Invert the cake onto a cake platter and tap it free. Brush off any loose crumbs.

7. Using a serrated knife, carefully cut the cake into three equal layers. Spoon one-third of the whipped cream on top of the bottom section and place one-third of the raspberries into the cream. Place the middle section on top. Spoon another one-third of the cream on the top and nestle half of the remaining raspberries into it. Place the third layer of cake on top and spoon the remaining cream over it. Arrange the raspberries decoratively into the cream and garnish with a sprig or two or leaves of fresh mint. Serve immediately.

Fresh Fruit Cobbler

Cobblers are the perfect casual dessert, especially in the summer, when markets are brimming with peaches, plums, cherries, and berries. I particularly like a peach-blueberry combination, but almost any stone fruit or berry does the trick. With a dollop of cold vanilla ice cream on the warm cobbler, heaven is just around the corner.

SERVES 6 TO 8

4 cups very ripe chopped peaches, plums, and/or whole berries

1 cup sugar

1 large egg, beaten

2 tablespoons cornstarch

1 teaspoon ground cinnamon, nutmeg, or ginger, optional

1 teaspoon fresh lemon juice

2 tablespoons unsalted butter, melted

Sweet Biscuit Dough (recipe follows)

1. Preheat the oven to 400°F. Generously butter a 2-quart casserole or a 9-inch square baking dish. Set aside.

2. Combine the fruit and sugar in a bowl. When the sugar has begun to dissolve, stir in the egg, cornstarch, optional spice, and the lemon juice. Stir in the melted butter and immediately pour the mixture into the prepared pan.

3. Drop the biscuit dough on the top of the fruit mixture by the tablespoonful, until the fruit is largely covered. Bake for 40 minutes, or until the top is lightly browned and the fruit is bubbling.

4. Serve warm (you can make the cobbler early in the day and reheat in a low oven just before serving) with vanilla ice cream, yogurt, whipped cream, or any light dessert sauce.

NOTE: For a fancier dessert, bake 8 individual cobblers in 8-ounce soufflé dishes. Place each dish on a serving plate and dust confectioners' sugar over the entire plate.

Sweet Biscuit Dough
MAKES ENOUGH FOR 1 COBBLER OR ABOUT 12 LARGE OR 24 SMALL SHORTCAKES

2 cups all-purpose flour
1 tablespoon plus 1 teaspoon baking powder
3 tablespoons sugar
8 tablespoons (1 stick) chilled unsalted butter or solid vegetable shortening, or a
    combination
¾ cup cold milk

1. Place the flour, baking powder, and sugar in the bowl of a food processor. Add the butter and pulse until the mixture is crumbly. Pour in the milk with the motor running and process quickly into a soft dough.

2. *For a cobbler topping*, drop the dough by the tablespoonful onto the fruit filling. Bake as directed in the individual recipe.

3. *For shortcakes*, roll the dough out to about a ½-inch thickness on a lightly floured board. Using a biscuit cutter or a glass (3 inches in diameter for large or 1½ inches for small biscuits), cut the dough into circles. Bake as directed in the individual recipe.

Strawberry Shortcake

Berry picking at one of the very few still-thriving farms on the eastern end of Long Island is a staple Palmer family outing. Sometimes it seems that we have eaten more than we have in our take-home baskets. This is our standard Fourth of July finish and somehow it always tastes better with big, fat juicy berries that we have picked ourselves.

6 cups (about 3 pints) sliced very ripe strawberries

½ cup granulated sugar, or to taste

1 teaspoon grated orange zest

6 large or 12 small biscuits made from Sweet Biscuit Dough (page 215)

1 cup heavy cream, well chilled

3 tablespoons confectioners' sugar

1 teaspoon pure vanilla extract

6 sprigs fresh mint

1. Combine the strawberries, granulated sugar, and orange zest in a large bowl. Using a kitchen fork, slightly mash about half of the berries. Let the berries macerate, at room temperature, for at least 1 hour.

2. Preheat the oven to 400°F.

3. Roll out the dough and cut out shortcake biscuits (see page 215). Place on a baking sheet and bake for about 15 minutes, or until lightly browned on top and cooked through.

4. With an electric mixer on low speed, beat the cream slightly in a chilled mixing bowl. Add the confectioners' sugar and vanilla and beat on high speed until the cream holds its shape but doesn't form stiff peaks. Refrigerate until ready to serve, but for no more than 15 minutes. (If you need to make the whipped cream early in the day, add ½ teaspoon unflavored gelatin dissolved in a teaspoon of warm water to the cream as you whip. The gelatin will enable the cream to hold its form.)

5. When ready to serve, split the biscuits crosswise in half. Place the bottoms of the biscuits, 1 large or 2 small per serving, in dessert plates. Spoon a generous serving of strawberries over the bottom half of each biscuit. Place the tops over the berries and spoon the remaining berries over the top and around the edges of the plates. Spoon a generous portion of whipped cream over the top of each, garnish with a mint sprig, and serve immediately.

Oven-Roasted Fruit with Caramel Sauce

When the winter fruit selection offers nothing more than apples and pears, I turn to dried fruits and nuts. I poach mixed dried fruits with wine and spices and then roast the fruits together with some nuts to caramelize the sugar and bring out their deep flavor. I top it all off with some homemade caramel sauce.

An easy make-ahead dessert; the fruit can be poached up to a week in advance and stored, covered, in the refrigerator. Roast the fruit before serving. Or if you don't get around to roasting the poached fruit, serve it with some vanilla yogurt, frozen or not, or ice cream.

SERVES 6

1½ pounds mixed dried fruit (peaches, pears, prunes, apples, figs, and/or apricots)

½ cup raisins

2 cups dry white wine

1 teaspoon minced fresh ginger

10 cloves

4 star anise

1 cinnamon stick

1 cup walnut halves, hazelnuts, or pine nuts

3 tablespoons unsalted butter, melted

Caramel Sauce (recipe follows)

1. Place the dried fruit and raisins in a heatproof bowl and cover with boiling water. Allow to stand for 30 minutes, or until the fruit has plumped. Drain off all the soaking liquid, reserving 1 cup.

2. Place the fruit and the reserved soaking liquid in a large saucepan. Add the wine, ginger, cloves, star anise, and cinnamon stick, place over medium heat, and bring to a boil. Immediately lower the heat to a low simmer, cover, and simmer for about 15 minutes, or until the fruit is quite soft. Remove from the heat and drain well, discarding the spices. (Reserve the poaching liquid for use in a marinade for pork or chicken, or for sauce, or to poach more dried or fresh fruit.)

3. Meanwhile, preheat the oven to 450°F.

4. Lightly butter a baking sheet. Spread the poached fruit and the nuts out on the baking sheet, leaving space between the fruit. Brush the tops with the melted butter. Roast for 10 minutes, or until the fruit is just beginning to color. Serve in individual bowls, drizzled with the caramel sauce.

Caramel Sauce

MAKES ABOUT 4 CUPS

1 cup packed light brown sugar
¾ cup granulated sugar
¼ cup corn syrup
1 tablespoon fresh lemon juice
1 tablespoon pure vanilla extract
1¾ cups heavy cream
2 tablespoons unsalted butter

1. Combine the brown and granulated sugars with 1 cup cold water in a heavy medium saucepan over medium heat and bring to a boil. Boil for 12 minutes, or until the syrup is a rich caramel color, brushing down the sides of the pan with a wet pastry brush from time to time to dissolve any sugar crystals that form.

2. Taking care as the syrup may bubble over, whisk in the corn syrup, lemon juice, and vanilla and bring to a simmer. Carefully whisk in the cream, bring to a boil, and boil gently for 10 minutes, or until the sauce is thick. Whisk in the butter and serve hot.

NOTE: This makes more sauce than you will need for the fruit, but you might as well make enough to have on hand for that late-night dish of (my favorite) coffee ice cream. The sauce will keep, tightly covered and refrigerated, for about 2 weeks. Reheat before serving.

My Favorite Chocolate Chip Cookies

F Ever since I was a little guy, these have been my favorite cookies. Anyone who knows me at all knows that a batch of chocolate chip cookies is the quickest way to my heart. My sons are now following in my footsteps with these cookies (neck-and-neck with the ever-popular Oreos), their snack-time favorites. Since they love to help make them, cookie baking is often our rainy day pastime.

As long as you're making this or any other cookie dough, make an extra batch and freeze it for Monday night football or a movie-watching night, when freshly baked cookies make the best half-time or intermission treat.

MAKES ABOUT 5 DOZEN

½ pound (2 sticks) unsalted butter, softened

1 cup packed dark brown sugar

½ cup granulated sugar

2 teaspoons pure vanilla extract

2 large eggs

2¼ cups all-purpose flour

2 tablespoons cocoa powder

½ teaspoon baking soda

¼ teaspoon baking powder

2½ cups semisweet or bittersweet chocolate chips (see Note)

1 to 1½ cups toasted pecan pieces (see Note)

1. Preheat the oven to 375°F. Lightly grease two or three cookie sheets or use nonstick cookie sheets.

2. Using an electric mixer, beat together the butter and sugars in a large bowl until light and fluffy, then beat in the vanilla. Beat in the eggs.

3. Combine the flour, cocoa, baking soda, and baking powder. With the mixer on low speed, beat the dry ingredients into the butter mixture until well blended. Fold in the chocolate chips and nuts until evenly distributed.

4. Using a kitchen teaspoon, drop the dough by the heaping spoonful onto the prepared cookie sheets, leaving about 2 inches between each cookie. Bake for about 10 minutes, or until the cookies are golden on top and lightly browned around the edges. Remove from the oven and allow to remain on the cookie sheets for about 3 minutes to set slightly. Using a spatula, lift the cookies onto wire racks to let cool.

5. Eat, as I do, while still warm, or let cool completely and store, tightly covered for soft cookies or loosely covered for crisp, for up to 3 days (but whoever keeps chocolate chip cookies that long?).

NOTE: I particularly love bittersweet chocolate chip cookies. If you want to try them and you can't find bittersweet chocolate bits, buy a pound block of bittersweet chocolate and chop it into tiny pieces.

Some people say that nuts are optional, but I have to have nuts in mine. If you don't like nuts, though, leave them out. If you do like them, be sure to toast them. You will find that the nuts will stay crunchier when they are baked in the cookie dough.

To make real chocolaty chocolate chip cookies, replace ¼ cup of the flour with ¼ cup Dutch-processed cocoa powder. You can also add ¾ cup unsweetened coconut flakes or ½ cup raisins, dried cranberries, or dried cherries to the basic recipe for a different twist on the old favorite.

Brownie–Ice Cream Sandwiches

These are right next to chocolate chip cookies as the number one favorite dessert for my boys—brownies and ice cream all in one bite. If you bake the brownies in one 8-inch square pan, they will be thicker and can be cut into bar cookies. Bake them in a 10-inch or larger pan if you want very thin sandwiches. Nuts or not, it's your choice, but, for me, brownies just aren't brownies without the crunch of nuts. Vanilla is our preferred ice cream, but coffee, chocolate chip, or any favorite flavor can be used.

MAKES 9

½ pound (2 sticks) unsalted butter, softened

2 cups sugar

4 large eggs

2 teaspoons pure vanilla extract

1 cup sifted all-purpose flour

½ cup unsweetened cocoa powder

1 cup walnut or pecan pieces, coarsely chopped, or macadamia nuts

2 to 3 pints vanilla ice cream, slightly softened

1. Preheat the oven to 350°F. Grease and flour two 9-inch square baking pans. Set aside.

2. Beat the butter and sugar in a large bowl with an electric mixer until light and fluffy. Beat in the eggs and vanilla. Sift the flour and cocoa into the bowl and beat until very well blended. Stir in the nuts. Scrape the batter into the prepared pans.

3. Bake the brownies for about 25 minutes, or until a toothpick inserted into the center comes out clean. Remove from the oven and cool on wire racks for 15 minutes. Cut into 3-inch squares and let cool completely in the pans.

4. When the brownies are cool, remove them from the pans. Carefully trim a thin slice off the bottom of each brownie (see Note). Turn 9 of the brownies trimmed side up. Working quickly and using a small spatula, cover the tops with ice cream. Place the remaining brownies trimmed side down on top. Individually wrap each sandwich in plastic and place in the freezer for at least 30 minutes to firm. Serve straight from the freezer.

NOTE: Crumble the brownie trimmings and mix them into ice cream or frozen yogurt or sprinkle them onto a frosted cake or cupcakes. If you don't want to use them right away, place the crumbs in a resealable plastic bag, label with the contents and date, and freeze them.

Pumpkin Custard with Ginger Cookies

If you and your gang are tired of pumpkin pie, try this rich, sweetly spiced alternative. You can bake it in one large dish for family meals or in individual soufflé dishes when company is expected. Since the custard can be served either warm or chilled, get your dessert making out of the way early in the day or even the night before.

SERVES 6

1 tablespoon unsalted butter

3 tablespoons chopped pecans

2 tablespoons minced crystallized ginger

1 tablespoon light brown sugar

1½ cups heavy cream

1 cup milk

One 3-inch piece vanilla bean, split

3 large eggs

2 large egg yolks

½ cup superfine sugar (see page 206)

½ teaspoon ground ginger

¼ teaspoon ground cinnamon

Pinch of ground cloves

⅔ cup well-drained canned pumpkin puree (see Note)

Whipped cream for serving, optional

Ginger Cookies (recipe follows)

1. Melt the butter in a small sauté pan over medium heat. Add the pecans and crystallized ginger and sauté for 4 min-

utes, or until the pecans are glazed with butter. Remove from the heat and spread the mixture over the bottom of a 2-quart deep casserole, or divide it among six small (8-ounce) soufflé dishes or ramekins. Sprinkle with the brown sugar. Place the casserole in a large shallow baking dish or place the dishes in a shallow baking dish large enough to hold them without crowding.

2. Preheat the oven to 325°F.

3. Combine the heavy cream and milk in a heavy medium saucepan over medium heat. Scrape the seeds from the vanilla bean into the cream mixture. Bring just to the boil and immediately remove from the heat.

4. Beat the eggs and egg yolks in a medium bowl with an electric mixer until well blended. Add the sugar and continue beating until pale yellow and thick. Beat in the ginger, cinnamon, and cloves. Beating continuously, pour the cream-milk mixture into the eggs in a slow, steady stream. Beat in the pumpkin puree until smooth. Pour into the prepared dish(es). Pour enough boiling water into the baking dish to come halfway up the sides of the dish(es).

5. Bake a large custard for about 40 minutes (or bake small individual custards for about 30 minutes), or until the custard is set in the center and the top is golden. Remove from the oven and let stand for about 30 minutes before serving warm, or let cool completely and serve chilled, in the baking dish(es) or unmolded (see Note). Garnish with whipped cream, if desired, and serve with the cookies on the side.

NOTE: Drain the pumpkin puree in a cheesecloth-lined fine sieve set over a bowl for 1 hour to remove some of its liquid.

To unmold individual custards, place each dish in about 1 inch of boiling water for 20 seconds. Place a serving plate over the top of the dish and quickly invert the custard onto it.

Ginger Cookies

MAKES ABOUT 5 DOZEN

½ cup packed dark brown sugar

½ cup granulated sugar

12 tablespoons (1½ sticks) butter, melted

2 large eggs

½ cup chopped walnuts or pecans

¼ cup finely minced crystallized ginger

Approximately 2⅓ cups sifted all-purpose flour

1 teaspoon baking soda

1 teaspoon ground cinnamon

1 teaspoon ground ginger

¼ teaspoon ground nutmeg

¼ teaspoon ground cloves

½ teaspoon salt

1. Combine the sugars with the melted butter in a large bowl and beat with an electric mixer until well blended. Add the eggs one at a time, beating well after each addition. Beat in the chopped nuts and crystallized ginger.

2. Sift together 2⅓ cups flour, the baking soda, cinnamon, ginger, nutmeg, cloves, and salt. Add to the sugar mixture and beat to just combine. The dough should be firm; add a bit more flour if necessary.

3. Form the dough into easy-to-handle rolls 1½ inches in diameter. Wrap the rolls in plastic wrap and refrigerate for at least 12 hours. (The dough can be frozen for up to 6 months; thaw in the refrigerator before baking.)

4. Preheat the oven to 325°F. Grease two or three cookie sheets.

5. Slice the rolls into ¼-inch-thick slices and place the cookies about 1 inch apart on the prepared cookie sheets. Bake for about 12 minutes, or until lightly browned. Remove from the pans and cool on wire racks. (The cookies can be stored, tightly covered, for up to 1 week.)

Brioche Bread Pudding

To me, warm bread pudding with vanilla ice cream melting into it is the most memory-provoking dessert. It takes me back to my mom's kitchen with its frosty windowpanes and the wood-burning stove. Since bread pudding is also good when cold, it makes a perfect see-you-through-the-weekend dessert. Warm the first night, chilled with some fruit sauce the second, and, hopefully, a bit left over for a snack during the week. For a grown-up presentation, add a few tablespoons of bourbon, rum, brandy, or fruit liqueur to the milk.

SERVES 8

4 tablespoons (½ stick) unsalted butter, softened

2 loaves (about 1½ pounds) brioche (or rich egg bread), cut into pieces

1 cup golden raisins and/or diced dried apricots, optional

4 cups half-and-half

4 large eggs

1½ cups sugar

1 tablespoon pure vanilla extract

1 teaspoon grated lemon zest

1 teaspoon ground cinnamon

1. Using the softened butter, generously butter a 13 × 9-inch glass baking dish. Toss the bread with the raisins and apricots, if using, then tightly pack the brioche into the pan.

2. Beat together the half-and-half and eggs in a large bowl. Beat in the sugar, vanilla, lemon zest, and cinnamon and beat

until the sugar is dissolved. Pour the liquid over the bread, patting it down with a spatula to make sure that all of the liquid will be soaked up by the bread. Cover with plastic wrap and let stand for 1 hour.

3. Preheat the oven to 350°F.

4. Unwrap the pudding and bake for about 1 hour, or until the top is golden brown and slightly puffed up. Remove from the oven and let rest for 10 minutes.

5. Cut the bread pudding into squares and serve, if desired, with whipped cream, ice cream or frozen yogurt, or any butter-based dessert sauce.

Pineapple Upside-down Cake

When winter has set in and the supermarket bins are laden with rock-hard, tasteless fruit and even the apples and pears are no longer appealing—it is time to pull out that can of pineapple that's been sitting on the shelf for just such a moment. Upside-down cakes are easy, last-minute desserts for weekdays and weekends. They are best made in a cast-iron skillet, but a 9-inch round or square cake pan will also do the trick.

MAKES ONE 9-INCH CAKE

4 tablespoons (½ stick) unsalted butter

1 cup packed light brown sugar

7 canned pineapple slices (one 20-ounce can), well drained

7 candied, dried, or maraschino cherries, optional

½ cup walnut or pecan halves

3 large eggs, separated

1½ cups granulated sugar

1 teaspoon pure vanilla extract

1½ cups sifted all-purpose flour

1½ teaspoons baking powder

1. Preheat the oven to 350°F.

2. Melt the butter in a 9-inch cast-iron skillet (or a 9-inch round or square cake pan) over low heat. Stir in the brown sugar and stir until the sugar has begun to dissolve and the mixture is well combined. Remove from the heat and quickly arrange the pineapple rings in a neat pattern in the pan. Place a cherry in the center of each ring, if desired, and scat-

ter the nuts over any empty spaces. Cover loosely with aluminum foil to keep warm.

3. Beat the egg yolks and granulated sugar in a large bowl with an electric mixer until thick and lemon colored. Beat in the vanilla. Sift the flour and baking powder together and alternately add to the egg mixture with ½ cup water, beating until very well blended.

4. Beat the egg whites in a medium bowl until stiff peaks form, then fold the beaten whites into the batter. Pour the batter over the pineapple in the prepared pan.

5. Bake for 25 to 30 minutes, or until a cake tester inserted into the center comes out clean. Remove from the oven and cool on a wire rack for 10 minutes. Invert onto a cake plate and gently tap the cake out. (It should release easily with the pineapple pattern in place.)

6. Serve hot or warm, with whipped cream or vanilla yogurt, ice cream, or frozen yogurt, if desired.

Ginger-Peach Ice Cream

The zing of the spicy ginger adds just the right contrast to the sweet aromatic peaches, making a perfectly balanced frozen treat. You can only make this ice cream in the height of the peach season, as you need the fragrance of ripe, juicy peaches to stand up to the ginger. For an extra-special dessert, serve this on top of freshly baked ginger-bread.

MAKES ABOUT 1 QUART

3 cups chopped peeled very ripe peaches

2 cups warm heavy cream

8 large egg yolks

¾ cup sugar, or to taste (see Note)

1 teaspoon pure vanilla extract

¾ cup finely chopped crystallized ginger

1. Combine the peaches and the warm cream in a food processor fitted with the metal blade. Depending upon your preference, either process until smooth or just pulse until the peaches are coarsely chopped.

2. Combine the egg yolks, sugar, and vanilla in a medium saucepan over medium-low heat. As soon as the mixture is well combined, whisk in the peach mixture. Cook, stirring constantly, for about 10 minutes, or until the custard coats the back of a spoon; do not boil. If you have pureed the peaches, strain the custard through a fine sieve to eliminate any lumps that might have formed.

3. Stir the crystallized ginger into the custard. Transfer to a nonreactive container with a lid. Cover and refrigerate for at least 2 hours and up to 24 hours, until well chilled.

4. Place the custard in an ice cream maker and freeze according to the manufacturer's directions.

NOTE: If the peaches are very sweet, you may not need all of the sugar. Add about ½ cup and taste before adding the remainder.

Sources

Specialty Foods, Cheeses, and Gourmet Groceries

Citarella
2135 Broadway
New York, NY 10023
(212) 874-0383

Dean & DeLuca
560 Broadway
New York, NY 10012
(800) 221–7714
www.deananddeluca.com

Fresh and Wild
P.O. Box 2981
Vancouver, WA 98668
(800) 222–5578

Gourmet Market
www.gourmetmarket.com
(800) 913–9247

MUSHROOMS
Mr. Mushroom
www.mushroom.com

Zabar's
2245 Broadway
New York, NY 10024
(212) 787–2000
www.zabars.com

Zingerman's
422 Detroit Street
Ann Arbor, MI 48104
(888) 636–8162
www.zingermans.com

Fish and Shellfish

Browne Trading Corporation
260 Commercial Street
Portland, ME 04101
(800) 944–7848
www.Browne-Trading.com

235

Marinelli Shellfish
Pier 33–Space L-17
The Embarcadero
San Francisco, CA 94111
(206) 810-0233

Seafood.com
430 Marrett Road
Lexington, MA 02421
(781) 861–1760
www.seafood.com

Specialty Meats and Game

D'Artagnan
399–419 Saint Paul Avenue
Jersey City, NJ 07306
(800) DAR–TAGN or (201) 792–0748
www.dartagnan.com

Niman Ranch
1025 East 12th Street
Oakland, CA 94606
(510) 808–0330
www.nimanranch.com

Kitchen Equipment

Bridge Kitchenware
214 East 52nd Street
New York, NY 10022
(212) 688–4220
bridgekitchenware.com

Chef's Catalog
3215 Commercial Avenue
Northbrook, IL 60062
(800) 825–8255
www.chefscatalog.com

Specialty Produce

Freida's Rare and Exotic Foods
P.O. Box 58488
Los Angeles, CA 90058
(800) 241–1771
www.freidas.com

Indian Rock Produce
Box 317
530 Quakertown Road
Quakertown, PA 18951
(800) 882–0512

Index

Aïoli:
  chicken salad, 63–64
  citrus, 64
anchovies, in tuna melts—my way, 80–81
angel food cake with raspberries and
    cream, 212–13
apple(s):
  cider–baked winter squash and,
    119–20
  "pizza" with cider sorbet, 207–8
  in Waldorf salad, 52–53
apple–corn relish, grilled marinated quail
    with, 155–57
applesauce, spicy, stuffed roasted pork loin
    with, 180–82
apricots, dried, in dried fruit and nut
    stuffing, 121–22
artichoke(s):
  hearts, chopped, in frittata, 82–83
  salmon salad with baby spinach, pea
    shoots and, 60–61
arugula, in roasted wild mushroom salad,
    44–45
Asian marinade, grilled pork tenderloin
    with, 178–79
asparagus:
  bow ties tossed with pancetta and,
    126–27
  in flank steak with grilled vegetables,
    160–61
  in frittata, 82–83
  in leg of lamb with spring vegetables,
    168–70

and spring onions, grilled, with mustard
    vinaigrette, 108–9
avocado salsa, 59

Baked:
  goat cheese, watercress with toasted
    walnuts and, 48–49
  lemon chicken, 145–46
  potatoes, 104
barbecued chicken, Mom's, 143–44
basil, capellini with fresh tomatoes and,
    128–29
bass, striped, whole roasted, with tarragon
    and shallots, 193–94
bean(s):
black, dried, in venison chili, 97–98
  white, and tuna salad, 56–57
beef:
  flank steak with grilled vegetables,
    160–61
  in great burgers on the grill, 72–73
  and peanut salad, Thai, 65–66
  perfect pot roast, 162–63
  roast, in one great big salad, 40–41
  roast, with Yorkshire pudding, 164–65
  in speidies, 100–101
beet(s):
  and garlic, roasted, 106
  in one great big salad, 40–41
  yellow, snow pea, and jícama salad,
    54–55
  yellow, in winter–vegetable shepherd's
    pie, 93–94

best butternut squash soup, 16–17
biscuit dough, sweet, 215
black beans, dried, in venison chili,
    97–98
black olive(s):
    in tuna melts—my way, 80–81
    vinaigrette, 62
blue cheese dressing, 77
Boston lettuce, in yellow beet, snow pea,
    and jícama salad, 54–55
bow ties tossed with asparagus and
    pancetta, 126–27
bread, 8–9
bread pudding, brioche, 228–29
breast of duck with citrus sauce and mixed
    fruit chutney, 151–53
brioche bread pudding, 228–29
broccoli, in frittata, 82–83
brown butter, sautéed soft–shell crabs
    with, 195–96
brownie–ice cream sandwiches, 223–24
brussels sprouts, sautéed, with pancetta,
    114–15
bulkie, crispy oysters and citrus
    mayonnaise on, 78–79
burgers on the grill, great, 72–73
butter:
    brown, sautéed soft–shell crabs with,
        195–96
    clarified, 8
butter lettuce, in lobster club sandwich,
    74–75
butternut squash soup, best, 16–17

Cake:
    angel food, with raspberries and cream,
        212–13
    chocolate–chocolate chip, 210–11
    pineapple upside–down, 230–31
capellini with fresh tomatoes and basil,
    128–29
caramelized turnips, venison chops with
    zinfandel sauce and, 183–85

caramel sauce, oven–roasted fruit with,
    218–19
carrots in Guinness, 107
cauliflower, in frittata, 82–83
celery rémoulade, 46–47
chanterelles, corn pudding with shaved
    Parmesan and, 111–13
Charlie's famous corn chowder, 12–13
cheddar cheese, sharp:
    in cheese strata, 91–92
    in green tomato tart, 84–85
    white, in super macaroni and cheese,
        123–24
cheese:
    cheez sammiches, 68–69
    in great burgers on the grill, 72–73
    in one great big salad, 40–41
    strata, 91–92
    super macaroni and, 123–24
    see also specific cheeses
cheez sammiches, 68–69
cherry tomatoes, in speidies, 100–101
chicken:
    barbecued, Mom's, 143–44
    carving of, 139
    fricassee with dumplings, 147–48
    in great burgers on the grill, 72–73
    lemon baked, 145–46
    noodle soup, Mom's, 34–35
    in one great big salad, 40–41
    perfect roast, 138–40
    salad, aïoli, 63–64
    in speidies, 100–101
chicken stock, 34–35
chili, venison, 97–99
chipotle chiles in adobo, in venison chili,
    97–98
chocolate chip:
    –chocolate cake, 210–11
    cookies, my favorite, 221–22
chowder, Charlie's famous corn, 12–13
chutney, mixed fruit, breast of duck with
    citrus sauce and, 151–54

cider–baked winter squash and apples, 119–20
cider sorbet, apple "pizza" with, 207–9
citrus aïoli, 64
    in aïoli chicken salad, 63–64
    in lobster club sandwich, 74–75
citrus mayonnaise and crispy oysters on a bulkie, 78–79
citrus sauce, breast of duck with mixed fruit chutney and, 151–53
clams, in fish soup with rouille and Parmesan toasts, 28–29
clarified butter, 8
club sandwich, lobster, 74–75
coconut milk, in grilled marinated quail with apple–corn relish, 155–56
composed salad of fennel, oven–dried pears, and Maytag blue cheese, 50–51
cookies:
    ginger, pumpkin custard with, 225–27
    my favorite chocolate chip, 221–22
corn:
    chowder, Charlie's famous, 12–13
    on the cob three ways, 110
    pudding with chanterelles and shaved Parmesan, 111–13
    in summer vegetable minestrone with pesto, 14–15
corn–apple relish, grilled marinated quail with, 155–56
country ham, 176–77
crab(s):
    boil, San Francisco, 199–200
    cakes, Maryland, 197–98
    soft–shell, sautéed, with brown butter, 195–96
cranberry beans, in summer vegetable minestrone with pesto, 14–15
cream, angel food cake with raspberries and, 212–13
creamy potato soup, 18–19
crème fraîche, 8
    in Waldorf salad, 52–53

crispy oysters and citrus mayonnaise on a bulkie, 78–79
custard, pumpkin, with ginger cookies, 225–26

Dandelion greens, baby, in roasted wild mushroom salad, 44–45
desserts, 203–33
    angel food cake with raspberries and cream, 212–13
    apple "pizza" with cider sorbet, 207–8
    brioche bread pudding, 228–29
    brownie–ice cream sandwiches, 223–24
    chocolate–chocolate chip cake, 210–11
    fresh fruit cobbler, 214–15
    ginger–peach ice cream, 232–33
    lemon meringue pie, 204–5
    my favorite chocolate chip cookies, 221–22
    oven–roasted fruit with caramel sauce, 218–19
    pineapple upside–down cake, 230–31
    pumpkin custard with ginger cookies, 225–26
    strawberry shortcake, 216–17
dough:
    pizza, 87–88
    sweet biscuit, 215
dressing, blue cheese, 77
dried apricots, in dried fruit and nut stuffing, 121–22
dried fruit and nut stuffing, 121–22
duck, breast of, with citrus sauce and mixed fruit chutney, 151–53
dumplings, chicken fricassee with, 147–48
Dungeness crabs, in San Francisco crab boil, 199–200

Easy gazpacho, 26–27
eggplant:
    in flank steak with grilled vegetables, 160–62
    ragù, linguine with, 130–31

eggs:

in frittata, 82–83

hard–boiled, in potato salad, 42–43

in Mom's barbecued chicken, 143–44

in roast beef with Yorkshire pudding, 164–65

Emmenthaler cheese, in potato–turnip gratin, 89–90

English muffins, in tomato–goat cheese melts, 70–71

Fennel:

composed salad of oven–dried pears, Maytag blue cheese and, 50–51

orange–braised, with hazelnuts, 118

saffron–mussel soup with, 32–33

fish and seafood:

crispy oysters and citrus mayonnaise on a bulkie, 78–79

fish soup with rouille and Parmesan toasts, 28–29

lobster club sandwich, 74–75

Maryland crab cakes, 197–98

mile–high shrimp sandwiches, 76–77

pan–roasted lobster with savory rice pilaf, 201–2

saffron–mussel soup with fennel, 32–33

salmon cakes with herbed tartar sauce, 190–91

salmon salad with baby spinach, pea shoots, and artichokes, 60–61

San Francisco crab boil, 199–200

sautéed soft–shell crabs with brown butter, 195

scallop and oyster stew, 95–96

tomatoes stuffed with shrimp salad, 58–59

tuna and white bean salad, 56–57

tuna melts—my way, 80–81

whole roasted salmon with new potatoes and leeks, 188–89

whole roasted striped bass with tarragon and shallots, 193–94

flaky pie pastry, 205–6

in green tomato tart, 84–85

flank steak with grilled vegetables, 160–61

Fontina cheese:

in super macaroni and cheese, 123–24

in tuna melts—my way, 80–81

fresh fruit cobbler, 214–15

fresh herbs, 7

fresh snap pea soup, 24–25

frittata, 82

fruit:

dried, and nut stuffing, 121–22

fresh, cobbler, 214–15

mixed, chutney, breast of duck with citrus sauce and, 151–54

oven–roasted, with caramel sauce, 218–19

Garlic:

and beets, roasted, 106

grilled leg of lamb with herbs and, 170–71

roasted, see roasted garlic

gazpacho, easy, 26–27

ginger cookies, pumpkin custard with, 225–27

ginger–peach ice cream, 232–33

goat cheese:

baked, watercress with toasted walnuts and, 48–49

crumbled, in green tomato tart, 84–85

–tomato melts, 70–71

golden raisins, in dried fruit and nut stuffing, 121–22

Granny Smith apples, in stuffed roasted pork loin with spicy applesauce, 180–82

grapes, seedless red, in Waldorf salad,
52–53
gratin, potato–turnip, 89–90
gravy, for perfect roast chicken,
138–40
great burgers on the grill, 72–73
greens:
mixed, in one great big salad,
40–41
sautéed, with red wine vinegar and
roasted shallots, 116–17
green tomato tart, 84–85
grill, great burgers on the, 72–73
grilled:
asparagus and spring onions with
mustard vinaigrette, 108–9
corn, 110
leg of lamb with herbs and roasted
garlic, 170–71
marinated quail with apple–corn relish,
155–56
pork tenderloin with Asian marinade,
178–79
vegetables, flank steak with,
160–61
ground beef, in great burgers on the grill,
72–73
Gruyère cheese:
in green tomato tart, 84–85
in onion soup in the French tradition,
20–21
Guinness, carrots in, 107

Ham:
in cheez sammiches, 68–69
in one great big salad, 40–41
two kinds of, 176–77
hash, turkey, 149–50
hash browns, 104
hazelnuts, orange–braised fennel with,
118
herbed tartar sauce, salmon cakes with,
190–92

herbs:
fresh, 7
grilled leg of lamb with roasted garlic
and, 170–71
honey–smoked turkey, 141–42

Ice cream:
–brownie sandwiches, 223–24
ginger–peach, 232–33

Jalapeño chile, in grilled marinated quail
with apple–corn relish, 155–56
jícama, yellow beet, and snow pea salad,
54–55

Lamb:
in great burgers on the grill, 72–73
leg of, grilled, with herbs and roasted
garlic, 170–71
leg of, with spring vegetables, 168–69
shanks with tomato, lentils and olives,
172–73
in speidies, 100–101
stew, light, 174–75
leeks:
melted, sage–seasoned roast loin of veal
with, 166–67
whole roasted salmon with new
potatoes and, 188–89
lemon:
chicken, baked, 145–46
meringue pie, 204–5
lentils, lamb shanks with tomato, olives
and, 172–73
lettuce:
Boston, in yellow beet, snow pea, and
jícama salad, 54–55
butter, in lobster club sandwich, 74–75
red oak leaf, in composed salad of fennel,
oven–dried pears, and Maytag blue
cheese, 50–51
light lamb stew, 174–75
linguine with eggplant ragù, 130–31

lobster:
    club sandwich, 74–75
    pan–roasted, with savory rice pilaf, 201–2

Macaroni and cheese, super, 123–24
marinade, Asian, grilled pork tenderloin
    with, 178–79
marinated quail, grilled, with apple–corn
    relish, 155–56
Maryland crab cakes, 197–98
mascarpone cheese, in super macaroni and
    cheese, 123–24
mashed potatoes, 105
    in winter–vegetable shepherd's pie,
    93–94
mayonnaise, citrus, 79
Maytag blue cheese:
    in blue cheese dressing, 77
    composed salad of fennel, oven–dried
    pears and, 50–51
melts:
    tomato–goat cheese, 70–71
    tuna, my way, 80–81
meringue, never–fail, in lemon meringue
    pie, 204–5
mile–high shrimp sandwiches, 76–77
minestrone with pesto, summer vegetable,
    14–15
mixed fruit chutney, 153–54
    breast of duck with citrus sauce and,
    151–53
Mom's barbecued chicken, 143–44
Mom's chicken noodle soup, 34–35
Monterey Jack cheese, in cheese strata,
    91–92
mushroom(s):
    button, in speidies, 100–101
    chanterelles, corn pudding with shaved
    Parmesan and, 111–13
    porcini, in pan–roasted lobster with
    savory rice pilaf, 201–2
    portobello, in flank steak with grilled
    vegetables, 160–61

portobello, in great burgers on the grill,
    72–73
soup (without cream), 22–23
in turkey soup with wild rice, 36–38
white, in sage–seasoned roast loin of
    veal with melted leeks, 166–67
wild, risotto, 134–35
wild, roasted, salad, 44–45
mussel(s):
    in fish soup with rouille and Parmesan
    toasts, 28–29
    –saffron soup with fennel, 32–33
mustard vinaigrette, grilled asparagus and
    spring onions with, 108–9
my favorite chocolate chip cookies, 221–22

Never–fail meringue, in lemon meringue
    pie, 204–5
new potatoes:
    in leg of lamb with spring vegetables,
    168–70
    in light lamb stew, 174–75
    in perfect pot roast, 162–63
    whole roasted salmon with leeks and,
    188–89
Niçoise olives, in pissaladière, 86–87
northern–style ham, 176–77
nut and dried fruit stuffing, 121–22

Olive(s):
    black, in tuna melts—my way, 80–81
    black, vinaigrette, 62
    lamb shanks with tomato, lentils and,
    172–73
    Niçoise, in pissaladière, 86–87
one great big salad, 40–41
onion(s):
    soup in the French tradition, 20–21
    spring, and asparagus, grilled, with
    mustard vinaigrette, 108–9
orange:
    –braised fennel with hazelnuts, 118
    –walnut vinaigrette, 49

oven–roasted:
    fruit with caramel sauce, 218–19
    potatoes, 105
oyster(s):
    crispy, and citrus mayonnaise on a
        bulkie, 78–79
    and scallop stew, 95–96

Pancetta:
    bow ties tossed with asparagus and,
        126–27
    sautéed brussels sprouts with,
        114–15
    in scallop and oyster stew, 95–96
pan–roasted lobster with savory rice pilaf,
    201–2
pappardelle with rabbit sauce, 132–33
Parmesan cheese:
    in frittata, 82–83
    shaved, corn pudding with chanterelles
        and, 111–13
    in wild mushroom risotto, 134
Parmesan toasts, fish soup with rouille
    and, 28–31
parsnips, in winter–vegetable shepherd's
    pie, 93–94
pasta, 125–35
    bow ties tossed with asparagus and
        pancetta, 126–27
    capellini with fresh tomatoes and basil,
        128–29
    linguine with eggplant ragù, 130–31
    pappardelle with rabbit sauce, 132–33
pastry, flaky pie, 205–6
peach–ginger ice cream, 232–33
peanut and Thai beef salad, 65–66
pears, oven–dried, composed salad of
    fennel, Maytag blue cheese and,
    50–51
peas, in summer vegetable minestrone
    with pesto, 14–15
pea shoots, salmon salad with baby
    spinach, artichokes and, 60–61

pecorino Romano cheese, in bow ties tossed
    with asparagus and pancetta, 126–27
peppers, roasted, 7
perfect pot roast, 162–63
perfect roast chicken, 138–40
pesto, summer vegetable minestrone with,
    14–15
pie:
    lemon meringue, 204–5
    shepherd's, winter–vegetable, 93–94
pie pastry, flaky, 205–6
pineapple upside–down cake, 230–31
pissaladière, 86–87
"pizza," apple, with cider sorbet, 207–8
pizza dough, 87–88
porcini mushrooms, in pan–roasted lobster
    with savory rice pilaf, 201–2
pork:
    in great burgers on the grill, 72–73
    loin, stuffed roasted, with spicy
        applesauce, 180–82
    in speidies, 100–101
    tenderloin, grilled, with Asian marinade,
        178–79
portobello mushrooms:
    in flank steak with grilled vegetables,
        160–61
    in great burgers on the grill, 72–73
potato(es), 104–5
    baked, 104
    in Charlie's famous corn chowder, 12–13
    cooked, in turkey hash, 149–50
    in frittata, 82–83
    hash browns, 104
    mashed, 105
    mashed, in winter–vegetable shepherd's
        pie, 93–94
    oven–roasted, 105
    soup, creamy, 18–19
    steamed, 104
    –turnip gratin, 89–90
    see also new potatoes
potato salad, 42–43

pot roast, perfect, 162–63
precooked ham, 176–77
pudding:
    brioche bread, 228–29
    corn, with chanterelles and shaved
        Parmesan, 111–13
    Yorkshire, roast beef with, 164–65
pumpkin custard with ginger cookies,
    225–26

Quail, grilled marinated, with apple–corn
    relish, 155–56

Rabbit sauce, pappardelle with, 132–33
radicchio, in flank steak with grilled
    vegetables, 160–61
ragù, eggplant, linguine with, 130–31
raisins, golden, in dried fruit and nut
    stuffing, 121–22
raspberries, angel food cake with cream
    and, 212–13
red oak leaf lettuce, in composed salad of
    fennel, oven–dried pears, and Maytag
    blue cheese, 50–51
red wine vinegar, sautéed greens with
    roasted shallots and, 116–17
relish, apple–corn, grilled marinated quail
    with, 155–57
rémoulade, celery, 46–47
rice, wild, turkey soup with, 36–38
rice pilaf, savory, pan–roasted lobster
    with, 201–2
ricotta salata cheese, in roasted wild
    mushroom salad, 44–45
risotto, wild mushroom, 134–35
roast:
    chicken, perfect, 138–40
    loin of veal, sage–seasoned, with
        melted leeks, 166–67
    turkey, 140
roast beef:
    in one great big salad, 40–41
    with Yorkshire pudding, 164–65

roasted:
    beets and garlic, 106
    corn, 110
    pork loin, stuffed, with spicy applesauce,
        180–82
    whole salmon with new potatoes and
        leeks, 188–89
    whole striped bass with tarragon and
        shallots, 193–94
    wild mushroom salad, 44–45
roasted garlic, 6–7
    in easy gazpacho, 26–27
    grilled leg of lamb with herbs and,
        170–71
    in honey–smoked turkey, 141–42
    in potato–turnip gratin, 89–90
    in stuffed roasted pork loin with spicy
        applesauce, 180–82
    in tuna and white bean salad, 56–57
    in tuna melts—my way, 80–81
    in turkey hash, 149–50
    in winter–vegetable shepherd's pie,
        93–94
roasted peppers, 7
rouille, fish soup with Parmesan toasts
    and, 28–31
rutabaga, in winter–vegetable shepherd's
    pie, 93–94

Saffron–mussel soup with fennel,
    32–33
sage–seasoned roast loin of veal with
    melted leeks, 166–67
salad dressings:
    avocado salsa, 59
    black olive vinaigrette, 62
    blue cheese dressing, 77
    citrus aïoli, 64
    orange–walnut vinaigrette, 49
    for Thai beef and peanut salad, 65–66
salads, 39–66
    aïoli chicken, 63–64
    celery rémoulade, 46–47

composed, of fennel, oven–dried pears,
and Maytag blue cheese, 50–51
one great big, 40–41
potato, 42–43
roasted wild mushroom, 44–45
salmon, with baby spinach, pea shoots,
and artichokes, 60–61
shrimp, tomatoes stuffed with, 58–59
Thai beef and peanut, 65–66
tuna and white bean, 56–57
Waldorf, 52–53
watercress with baked goat cheese and
toasted walnuts, 48–49
yellow beet, snow pea, and jícama, 54–55
salmon:
cakes with herbed tartar sauce, 190–91
salad with baby spinach, pea shoots, and
artichokes, 60–61
whole roasted, with new potatoes and
leeks, 188–89
salsa, avocado, 59
sandwiches:
brownie–ice cream, 223–24
cheez sammiches, 68–69
crispy oysters and citrus mayonnaise on
a bulkie, 78–79
goat cheese–tomato melts, 70–71
great burgers on the grill, 72–73
lobster club, 74–75
mile–high shrimp, 76–77
tuna melts—my way, 80–81
San Francisco crab boil, 199–200
sauce:
caramel, oven–roasted fruit with,
218–20
citrus, breast of duck with mixed fruit
chutney and, 151–53
herbed tartar, salmon cakes with,
190–92
rabbit, pappardelle with, 132–33
tomato, 125
zinfandel, venison chops with
caramelized turnips and, 183–85

sautéed:
brussels sprouts with pancetta, 114–15
greens with red wine vinegar and
roasted shallots, 116–17
soft–shell crabs with brown butter,
195–96
scallop and oyster stew, 95–96
seafood, *see* fish and seafood
serrano chile, in salmon cakes with herbed
tartar sauce, 190–91
shallots, roasted, sautéed greens with red
wine vinegar and, 116–17
shepherd's pie, winter–vegetable, 93–94
shortcake, strawberry, 216–17
shrimp:
in fish soup with rouille and Parmesan
toasts, 28–29
salad, tomatoes stuffed with shrimp,
58–59
sandwiches, mile–high, 76–77
snap pea soup, fresh, 24–25
snow pea, yellow beet, and jícama salad,
54–55
soft–shell crabs, sautéed, with brown
butter, 195–96
sorbet, cider, apple "pizza" with, 207–9
soup, 11–38
best butternut squash, 16–17
Charlie's famous corn chowder, 12–13
creamy potato, 18–19
easy gazpacho, 26–27
fish, with rouille and Parmesan toasts,
28–29
fresh snap pea, 24–25
Mom's chicken noodle, 34–35
mushroom (without cream), 22–23
onion, in the French tradition, 20–21
saffron–mussel, with fennel, 32–33
summer vegetable minestrone with
pesto, 14–15
turkey, with wild rice, 36–38
southern–style ham, 176–77
speidies, 100–101

spicy applesauce, stuffed roasted pork loin with, 180–82

spinach, baby, salmon salad with pea shoots, artichokes and, 60–61

spring onions and asparagus, grilled, with mustard vinaigrette, 108–9

spring vegetables, leg of lamb with, 168–69

squash:
    butternut, soup, best, 16–17
    summer, in frittata, 82–83
    winter, and apples, cider–baked, 119–20
    yellow, in summer vegetable minestrone with pesto, 14–15

steak, flank, with grilled vegetables, 160–61

steamed potatoes, 104

stew:
    lamb, light, 174–75
    scallop and oyster, 95–96

stocks, 6
    chicken, 34–35
    turkey, 36–38

strata, cheese, 91–92

strawberry shortcake, 216–17

striped bass, whole roasted, with tarragon and shallots, 193–94

stuffed roasted pork loin with spicy applesauce, 180–82

stuffing, dried fruit and nut, 121–22

summer squash, in frittata, 82–83

summer vegetable minestrone with pesto, 14–15

sun–dried tomatoes, in pissaladière, 86–87

super macaroni and cheese, 123–24

sweet biscuit dough, 215

Swiss chard, in winter–vegetable shepherd's pie, 93–94

Tart, green tomato, 84–85

tartar sauce, herbed, salmon cakes with, 190–92

Thai beef and peanut salad, 65–66

toasts, Parmesan, fish soup with rouille and, 28–31

tomato(es):
    canned, in venison chili, 97–98
    canned Italian plum, in linguine with eggplant ragù, 130–31
    cherry, in speidies, 100–101
    in easy gazpacho, 26–27
    fresh, capellini with basil and, 128–29
    –goat cheese melts, 70–71
    green, tart, 84–85
    lamb shanks with lentils, olives and, 172–73
    in one great big salad, 40–41
    stuffed with shrimp salad, 58–59
    in summer vegetable minestrone with pesto, 14–15
    sun–dried, in pissaladière, 86–87
    yellow or orange, in lobster club sandwich, 74–75

tomato sauce, 125

tuna:
    melts—my way, 80–81
    and white bean salad, 56–57

turkey:
    in great burgers on the grill, 72–73
    hash, 149–50
    honey–smoked, 141–42
    roasting of, 140
    soup with wild rice, 36–38
    in speidies, 100–101

turkey stock, 36–38

turnip(s):
    baby, in a light lamb stew, 174–75
    baby, in perfect pot roast, 162–63
    caramelized, venison chops with zinfandel sauce and, 183–85
    –potato gratin, 89–90

tiny, in leg of lamb with spring
vegetables, 168–70
two kinds of ham, 176–77

Veal, sage–seasoned roast loin of, with
melted leeks, 166–67
vegetables, 103–24
grilled, flank steak with, 160–61
spring, leg of lamb with, 168–69
summer, minestrone with pesto, 14–15
winter, shepherd's pie, 93–94
see also specific vegetables
venison:
chili, 97–99
chops with zinfandel sauce and
caramelized turnips, 183–85
vinaigrette:
black olive, 62
mustard, grilled asparagus and spring
onions with, 108–9
orange–walnut, 49
vinegar, red wine, sautéed greens with
roasted shallots and, 116–17

Waldorf salad, 52–53
walnut–orange vinaigrette, 49
walnuts, toasted, watercress with baked
goat cheese and, 48–49
watercress with baked goat cheese and
toasted walnuts, 48–49

white bean and tuna salad, 56–57
white mushrooms, in sage–seasoned
roast loin of veal with melted leeks,
166–67
whole roasted:
salmon with new potatoes and leeks,
188–89
striped bass with tarragon and shallots,
193–94
wild mushroom:
risotto, 134–35
salad, roasted, 44–45
wild rice, turkey soup with, 36–38
winter squash and apples, cider–baked,
119–20
winter–vegetable shepherd's pie, 93–94

Yellow beet(s):
snow pea, and jícama salad, 54–55
in winter–vegetable shepherd's pie,
93–94
yellow squash, in summer vegetable
minestrone with pesto, 14–15
Yorkshire pudding, roast beef with,
164–65

Zinfandel sauce, venison chops with
caramelized turnips and, 183–85
zucchini, in summer vegetable
minestrone with pesto, 14–15